TOPSY-TURVY

by the same author

screenplays
NAKED and other screenplays
SECRETS AND LIES
CAREER GIRLS

plays
ABIGAIL'S PARTY with GOOSE-PIMPLES (Penguin)
ECSTASY with SMELLING A RAT
(Nick Herne Books)

TOPSY-TURVY
Mike Leigh

faber and faber

First published in 1999
by Faber and Faber Limited
3 Queen Square London WC1N 3AU

Photoset by Parker Typesetting Service
Printed in England by Clays Ltd, St Ives plc

All rights reserved
© Mike Leigh, 1999

Stills © Simon Mein, 1999

Mike Leigh is hereby identified
as the author of this work in accordance
with Section 77 of the Copyright,
Designs and Patents Act 1988

*This book is sold subject to the condition that it shall not,
by way of trade or otherwise, be lent, resold, hired out or
otherwise circulated without the publisher's prior consent in
any form of binding or cover other than that in which it is
published and without a similar condition including this
condition being imposed on the subsequent purchaser*

A CIP record for this book is available
from the British Library

ISBN 0-571-20206-3

2 4 6 8 10 9 7 5 3 1

CONTENTS

Introduction by Mike Leigh, vii

TOPSY-TURVY, 1

The Music Cues, 138

INTRODUCTION

Topsy-Turvy is a film about all of us who suffer and strain to make other people laugh.

Gilbert and Sullivan dominated the musical theatre in the English-speaking world of a hundred years ago, and I have always been fascinated not only by their personalities but by the way in which they and their collaborators fought and struggled to produce such harmonious, delightful and profoundly trivial material.

The film is an attempt to evoke their world, and to bring it to life. For me, it is also somehow a last chance to glance briefly over my shoulder at the quickly receding past, before embarking on the imminent journey into the new century.

Mike Leigh
(Venice Film Festival Notes, 1999)

Credits

Topsy-Turvy was first shown at the Venice Film Festival on 3 September 1999. The cast and crew was as follows:

CAST IN ORDER OF APPEARANCE

ARTHUR SULLIVAN	Allan Corduner
LOUIS	Dexter Fletcher
CLOTHILDE	Sukie Smith
STAGE DOOR-KEEPER	Roger Heathcott
HELEN LENOIR	Wendy Nottingham
FRANK CELLIER	Stefan Bednarczyk
ARMOURER	Geoffrey Hutchings
RICHARD TEMPLE	Timothy Spall
BUTT	Francis Lee
COOK	William Neenan
SHRIMP	Adam Searle
GEORGE GROSSMITH	Martin Savage
WILLIAM SCHWENCK GILBERT	Jim Broadbent
LUCY GILBERT ('KITTY')	Lesley Manville
MRS JUDD	Kate Doherty
PIDGEON	Kenneth Hadley
MAIDSERVANT	Keeley Gainey
RICHARD D'OYLY CARTE	Ron Cook
FANNY RONALDS	Eleanor David
PIANIST IN BROTHEL	Gary Yershon
MADAME	Katrin Cartlidge
MADEMOISELLE FROMAGE	Julia Rayner
SECOND PROSTITUTE	Jenny Pickering
DURWARD LELY	Kevin McKidd
RICHARD BARKER	Sam Kelly
GILBERT'S FATHER	Charles Simon
PARIS WAITER	Philippe Constantin
DENTIST	David Neville
WALTER SIMMONDS	Matthew Mills
LEONORA BRAHAM	Shirley Henderson

MR SEYMOUR	Nicholas Woodeson
STAGE HANDS	Nick Bartlett
	Gary Dunnington
JESSIE BOND	Dorothy Atkinson
EMILY	Amanda Crossley
SPINNER	Kimi Shaw
CALLIGRAPHER	Toksan Takahashi
DANCER	Akemi Otani
SHAMISEN PLAYER	Kanako Morishita
MAUDE GILBERT	Theresa Watson
FLORENCE GILBERT	Lavinia Bertram
FIRST KABUKI ACTOR	Togo Igawa
SECOND KABUKI ACTOR	Eiji Kusuhara
MISS 'SIXPENCE PLEASE'	Naoko Mori
GILBERT'S MOTHER	Eve Pearce
BOY ACTOR	Neil Humphries
RUTLAND BARRINGTON	Vincent Franklin
FREDERICK BOVILL	Michael Simkins
MADAME LEON	Alison Steadman
SIBYL GREY	Cathy Sara
MISS MORTON	Angela Curran
ALICE	Millie Gregory
WILHELM	Jonathan Aris
JOHN D'AUBAN	Andy Serkis
MRS RUSSELL	Mia Soteriou
ROSINA BRANDRAM	Louise Gold
MR HARRIS	Shaun Glanville
MR PLANK	Julian Bleach
MR HURLEY	Neil Salvage
MR TRIPP	Matt Bardock
MAD WOMAN	Bríd Brennan

LADIES AND GENTLEMEN OF THE CHORUS

MR PRICE	Mark Benton
MISS RUSSELL	Heather Craney
MISS MEADOWS	Julie Jupp
MR SANDERS	John Warnaby

MISS FITZHERBERT	Kacey Ainsworth
MR MARCHMONT	Ashley Artus
MR GORDON	Richard Attlee
MR FLAGSTONE	Paul Barnhill
MR CONYNGHAM	Nicholas Boulton
MISS JARDINE	Lorraine Brunning
MR LEWIS	Simon Butteriss
MR RHYS	Wayne Cater
MISS MOORE	Rosie Cavaliero
MISS WARREN	Michelle Chadwick
MISS KINGSLEY	Debbie Chazen
MR HAMMOND	Richard Coyle
MISS BARNES	Monica Dolan
MISS BROWN	Sophie Duval
MISS BIDDLES	Anna Francolini
MISS COLEFORD	Teresa Gallagher
MISS WOODS	Sarah Howe
MISS TRINGHAM	Ashley Jensen
MISS LANGTON-JAMES	Gemma Page
MR BENTLEY	Paul Rider
MISS CARLYLE	Mary Roscoe
MR KENT	Steven Speirs
MISS BETTS	Nicola Wainwright
MISS WILKINSON	Angie Wallis
MR EVANS	Kevin Walton
Written and Directed by	Mike Leigh
Produced by	Simon Channing-Williams
Cinematography	Dick Pope BSC
Editor	Robin Sales
Music	Carl Davis from the works of Arthur Sullivan
Production Designer	Eve Stewart
Costume Designer	Lindy Hemming
Make-up and Hair Designer	Christine Blundell
Sound Recordist	Tim Fraser
Musical Director	Gary Yershon
Choreographer	Francesca Jaynes
Research	Rosie Chambers

Associate Producer   Georgina Lowe
Casting   Nina Gold

A Thin Man Film
with
The Greenlight Fund
and
Newmarket Capital Group

TOPSY-TURVY

Blank screen.
A man's voice.
MAN: One, two – two, two.

A solo piano, bright and brisk. Front credits start. Three young women sing.
WOMEN:
>So please you, Sir, we much regret
>If we have failed in etiquette
>Towards a man of rank so high –
>We shall know better by and by.

WOMAN 1:
>But youth, of course, must have its fling,
>So pardon us,
>So pardon us,

WOMAN 2:
>And don't, in girlhood's happy spring,
>Be hard on us,
>Be hard on us
>If we're inclined to dance and sing.
>Tra la la la la la.

ALL THREE WOMEN:
>But youth, of course, must have its fling,
>So pardon us,
>And don't, in girlhood's happy spring,
>Be hard on us.
>But youth, of course, must have its fling,
>So pardon us –
>Tra la la la la la la la la,
>Tra la la la la la la la,
>Tra la la la la la la la,
>Tra la la la la la la la,
>Tra la la la la la la la,
>La la la la la la!

Main title: 'TOPSY-TURVY'. Piano solo fades as we dissolve to a sea of empty blue theatre seats. A young man in a black suit and white gloves enters the second row and begins to work his way along, checking each seat by lowering it for a moment. Silence, except for the sound of the seats.

A caption:

                    'London, January 5th 1884.'

Credits continue. The camera cranes down and tilts up to reveal two more young men in black suits checking the stalls seats; then we crane up to the circle, where two further young men are performing the same task. The front of the circle is adorned with a festive floral arrangement.

Night. A man sits up in bed. He is in shock as though suddenly having woken from a bad dream. A clock on the mantelpiece is striking eight. The man, obviously in pain, focuses his thoughts. Then he throws back his bedclothes, grasps a large hand-bell, and starts ringing it violently. We hear somebody enter the room.
NEWCOMER (*German accent*): Sir Arthur, what are you doing?
SIR ARTHUR SULLIVAN: I'm going to the theatre, Louis.
LOUIS (*grasping* SULLIVAN): No, it is not possible –
SULLIVAN: I . . . have no choice!
LOUIS: You must get back into –
SULLIVAN: Louis!!!
    (*Pause. Then* LOUIS *leaves.* SULLIVAN *gasps for breath.*)

SULLIVAN's *corridor. Maroon, Moroccan-style.* LOUIS *walks briskly past a maidservant into a pantry*
LOUIS: Hot coffee – very strong, please.
    (*Music cue 1 starts.*)
MAID (*Belgian accent*): D'accord.
    (*She goes.* LOUIS *swiftly places several items including a towel on a tray. Then he returns to* SULLIVAN.)

In his bedroom, SULLIVAN *grimaces:* LOUIS *is injecting his thigh. He pulls out the needle and rubs* SULLIVAN's *skin with his bare hand.*

Minutes later, still in the bedroom. LOUIS *is shaving* SULLIVAN.
SULLIVAN: Louis –
LOUIS: Don't move –
SULLIVAN: *Schnell!!*
LOUIS: Please!

Now SULLIVAN, *standing in his dress shirt and tie, is draining a coffee-cup as* LOUIS *helps him on with his waistcoat.*
SULLIVAN: Clothilde, *encore du café – vite!*
CLOTHILDE (*taking the cup and saucer*): *Oui.*

SULLIVAN *rushes out of his apartment. He is wearing his top hat and cloak, and drinking from the coffee-cup as he goes.* LOUIS *has his arm round him for support.* CLOTHILDE *follows.*
CLOTHILDE: Sir Arthur, *la tasse, s'il vous plaît!*
    (*He gives it to her.*)
SULLIVAN: *D'accord.*
CLOTHILDE: *Bonne chance*, Sir Arthur!
SULLIVAN: *Merci.*

SULLIVAN *and* LOUIS *cross the landing (classical columns, oak panels, large plants) and rush down the wide staircase.*
LOUIS: *Nicht so schnell!*
SULLIVAN (*shaking free*): Louis! *Ich muss das allein tun* – I'll be
    fine. Now go and fetch the cab!
    (*Music cue 1 ends.* LOUIS *adjusts* SULLIVAN'*s cloak as they disappear down the stairs.*)

In the cab (a brougham). Snow falling. LOUIS *fastens* SULLIVAN'*s coat.* SULLIVAN, *eyes closed, looks ill.*
  (*Music cue 2 starts.*)

The cab pulls up in a side street. A few huddled passers-by. LOUIS *opens the cab's half-doors and alights.*

LOUIS *thrusts open a pair of double doors for* SULLIVAN *who rushes down a corridor. Without stopping, he taps with his cane on the counter of a hatch, in which sits a stage door keeper (*MANTON*) wearing a top hat.*

SULLIVAN: Manton!
MANTON (*surprised*): Good evening, sir!
> (*As* SULLIVAN *continues down the corridor,* LOUIS *helps him off with his hat and coat. On seeing* SULLIVAN, *a woman and a man, both in evening dress, come out of a room at the far end of the corridor.*)

WOMAN: Arthur!
MAN: Good God, Arthur, is this entirely wise?
SULLIVAN: No, it's entirely foolish, Frank.
WOMAN: D'you intend to go on?
SULLIVAN: I certainly do, Helen – I've never missed one yet.
HELEN: Very well, I'll let everybody know.

She rushes off. SULLIVAN *makes for a chair in the little room, and sits down.* FRANK (CELLIER, *Sullivan's musical director*) *takes a flask from a shelf, and gives it to* SULLIVAN.

CELLIER: Here – take a drink.
SULLIVAN: Thank you. (*He does so.*) Oh, that's better, Frank.
> (CELLIER *takes the flask. He puts a cigarette in* SULLIVAN's *mouth.*)

LOUIS: Gloves.
SULLIVAN: Thank you, Louis.
> (*He takes the white kid gloves, and puts them on.* CELLIER *drops a match on the floor, picks it up, strikes it, and lights* SULLIVAN's *cigarette.*)

CELLIER: This is a surprise!
SULLIVAN: Yes, you might say that!

The theatre, in the stalls. A full house – ladies and gentlemen in their evening dress. They chatter. SULLIVAN *appears. Everybody claps. Up in the gods, the lower-class folk rise to their feet and cheer.* SULLIVAN *settles into his chair, puts on his monocle, and holds up his baton. The applause dies down, and he conducts the overture to* Princess Ida. *There is now a twinkle in his eye. He is enjoying himself.*

A little later. The show is in progress. On stage, we hear the chorus of men and women sing.

CHORUS (*sings*):
> As up we string
> The faithless King
> In the old familiar way!
> We'll shout ha! ha! hip, hip, hurrah!
> Hip, hip, hip, hip, hurrah!
> As we make an end of her false papa
> Hurrah! Hurrah!
> (*During this, in the wings, a small, dapper man with a neatly trimmed beard adjusts the cumbersome mediaeval armour on two or three large actors wearing huge false beards. He is the* ARMOURER. *He is assisted by a youth in a bowler hat. Two actresses scuttle by.*)

*Meanwhile, in a corridor, a call-boy (*SHRIMP*) in a peaked cap rushes up to a gentleman dresser.*
SHRIMP (*saluting*): Permission, Mr Cook?
COOK (*saluting*): Permission, Shrimp.
   (SHRIMP *knocks on a dressing-room door.*)
MAN'S VOICE (*inside*): Come!
   (SHRIMP *opens the door. An actor, dressed and made up as a grotesque old man with a long, white beard, sits at his mirror.*)

SHRIMP: Five minutes, Mr Grossmith.
 (GROSSMITH *glares at* SHRIMP, *who closes the door and runs off.*)

SULLIVAN *conducts an introduction.* GROSSMITH *appears on stage between two guards. He looks round suspiciously, then he scuttles down to stage centre with his walking-stick. The* CHORUS *of ladies and gentlemen courtiers bow respectfully. The set is mediaeval romantic; all trees and arches and a distant classical portico. During the following,* SULLIVAN *enjoys the joke.*
GROSSMITH (*sings*):
 If you give me your attention, I will tell you what I am:
 I'm a genuine philanthropist – all other kinds are sham.
 Each little fault of temper and each social defect
 In my erring fellow-creatures I endeavour to correct.
 To all their little weaknesses I open people's eyes;
 And little plans to snub the self-sufficient I devise;
 I love my fellow-creatures – I do all the good I can –
 Yet everybody says I'm such a disagreeable man!
 And I can't think why!
 (*Several courtiers look askance. During part of the next verse, we cut to a* MAN *with a large moustache sitting on a sofa and*

smoking a cigar in a room somewhere in the theatre, within earshot of the stage. He looks agitated.)
GROSSMITH (*sings*):
   I'm sure I'm no ascetic; I'm as pleasant as can be;
   You'll always find me ready with a crushing repartee.
   I've an irritating chuckle, I've a celebrated sneer,
   I've an entertaining snigger, I've a fascinating leer.
   To everybody's prejudice I know a thing or two;
   I can tell a woman's age in half a minute – and I do,
   (*Two lady* CHORUS *members exchange appalled looks.*)
   And I can't think why!
CHORUS (*sings*):
   He can't think why!
   (*On the final note of the song,* GROSSMITH *kicks his leg – a comic 'attitude'.*)

The Savoy Theatre 'Green Room'. The ARMOURER *opens the door and comes in. He greets* W. S. GILBERT, *the agitated man with the cigar, who is still on the sofa. Down on the stage, the finale to* Princess Ida, *Act 2, can be heard.*
ARMOURER (*laughing*): Monsieur!
GILBERT (*aggressively*): Bonsoir.
   (*The* ARMOURER *picks up his hat and cane.*)
ARMOURER: Vous avez là un succès certain.
GILBERT: Merci.
ARMOURER (*leaving*): Au revoir!
   (*He has gone.*)
GILBERT: What d'you expect me to do? Kiss the carpenters?
   (*He puffs his cigar.*)

A group of people is walking along the stage door corridor. One of them collapses on the floor. It is SULLIVAN.
CELLIER: Arthur!
   (*Everybody attends to him. Much talking at once.* SULLIVAN *groans.*)
MAN: Let's get him up.
LOUIS: Come on, Sir Arthur.
   (SULLIVAN *groans again. They sit him up, against the wall.* CELLIER *produces the flask.*)

CELLIER: Arthur, take some brandy.
   (*He puts the flask to* SULLIVAN*'s lips.* GILBERT *arrives in his top hat.*)
GILBERT: What happened? What happened?
   (SULLIVAN *drinks and splutters.*)
LOUIS: He will be fine.
MAN: Is Dr Lynch in the house?

Next morning. GILBERT, *clutching a newspaper, and wearing his smoking-jacket and cap, strides purposefully through the hall of his house. He steams into the breakfast room. Three servants, a middle-aged butler, a housekeeper and a maidservant, wait in a line by the door. His wife is sitting at the table in her black riding apparel.* GILBERT *stands in front of a nautical portrait of himself, and addresses her.*

GILBERT: Listen to this . . . today's *Times*. (*He reads.*) *Princess Ida* will probably run for a year, keeping the Savoy treasury agreeably replete all the while. All London will flock to hear it. So will our provincial and American cousins and Continental visitors. Copies of its words and music will be sold by tens of thousands.

(MRS GILBERT *smiles.*)
Everybody connected with its performance will have a good time for at least a twelve-month to come. (*Addressing staff*) So mote it be!

MRS GILBERT (*cheerfully*) How splendid, Willie.

GILBERT: Sugared words, Lucy. Listen. (*He reads.*) The opera is above the level of all other entertainments before the London public. Still, I cannot pronounce it to be in any way an improvement upon its predecessors. To me, words and music alike reveal *symptoms of fatigue* in their respective composer and author. Arthur Sullivan cannot write other than in a pleasing manner, but more than one number in *Princess Ida* is lacking in the freshness and spontaneity of *The Pirates of Penzance, Patience, Iolanthe* or *The Sorcerer*, his best operatic work – Oh, *is it*??!! (*Reading.*) Or *HMS Pinafore*, the most popular. W. S. Gilbert abundantly proves he is still the legitimate monarch of the Realm of Topsy-Turvydom. (*To the maid and the housekeeper:*) Thank you very much!!
(*The maid looks nervously at the housekeeper, who is impassive. Gilbert continues reading.*)
But his incongruities are more elaborately worked up than of yore, and therefore less funny. Moreover, the story is a *dull one*. Burn it, Pidgeon!!
(*He thrusts the newspaper at the butler, and strides out of the room.*)

PIDGEON: Sir.
(LUCY *scuttles down the hall after* GILBERT.)

LUCY: Willie! Your kidneys are getting cold!!
(*The servants, still in a line, crane forward to watch their master and mistress disappear into a room at the far end of the hall.*)

SULLIVAN'*s bedroom. Day. Exotic décor – much green and gold. Peacock motifs on the door.* SULLIVAN *is sitting up in bed, wearing a smoking cap and sporting a cigarette in a holder. He has visitors.* RICHARD D'OYLY CARTE, *a dapper little man with a beard and a fur-collared overcoat, and* HELEN LENOIR, *the woman who greeted him on his arrival at the theatre.* CARTE *stands by the side of the bed, and* HELEN, *wearing a hat, sits at its foot on a chair.*

LOUIS *is pouring tea.*
CARTE: The show's doing splendidly, Arthur. Full houses and a healthy advance.
SULLIVAN: Capital!
CARTE: Three tours on the road: *Pirates, Patience* and *Iolanthe* –
HELEN: And four in rehearsal.
SULLIVAN: *Merveilleux.*
HELEN: New York can't wait for *Ida*.
SULLIVAN: Ah, New York. How splendid!
CARTE: Helen has us booked up to the end of the year.
SULLIVAN: Tireless as ever.
HELEN: All part of my day's work.
LOUIS: Tea, Miss Lenoir? (*He offers her a cup and saucer.*)
HELEN: No, thank you, Louis.
LOUIS: Very well.
  (SULLIVAN *is putting out his cigarette. Music cue 3 starts.*)
HELEN: I do hope your confinement hasn't made you restless, Arthur. How have you been passing the time?
SULLIVAN: I've made some resolutions, Helen.
  (CARTE *looks at him.*)
  A little late in the New Year, perhaps, but . . .
HELEN: Better late than never.
  (LOUIS *leaves the room. He has given* CARTE *his tea.*)
CARTE: May we know what they are, Arthur?
SULLIVAN: Why not? One: to travel to the Continent . . . as soon as my health permits.
CARTE: Very wise.
SULLIVAN: I think so. Two: to look for a country house where I may repair each summer, without having to cross the Channel. Three: to take more exercise.
CARTE: Excellent, Arthur, and about time, too.
SULLIVAN: A leaf out of your book, D'Oyly. I must walk more.
HELEN: And is there a number four?
SULLIVAN: Yes. To write no more operas for the Savoy.
  (*Pause.* CARTE *and* HELEN *exchange looks.*)
CARTE: And what is number five?
HELEN: To fly to the moon with his bedsocks on.
SULLIVAN: No, I'm serious. I have to write a grand opera. People expect it of me, I must not disappoint them. I

cannot waste any more time on these trivial soufflés. D'you know, I haven't written a symphony for over twenty years.
CARTE: Not an unprofitable twenty years, if I may say so.
(SULLIVAN *is affected by this comment.*)
HELEN: Arthur, if you would only learn to organize your time more efficiently, you could do everything you wished.
SULLIVAN: My time is finite, Helen. I must fill it with that which is important to me.
CARTE: Is not the Savoy Theatre important to you?
SULLIVAN: This work with Gilbert is quite simply killing me.
CARTE: Working with Gilbert would kill anybody.
(HELEN *half smiles; an amused grunt from* SULLIVAN.)
HELEN: Is your contract with D'Oyly and Mr Gilbert not important to you?
(CARTE *gets up quickly, and moves to the foot of the bed.* HELEN *joins him.*)
CARTE: But our present concern is your health. You must go to the South of France and recover. We can discuss this on your return.
SULLIVAN: I shall recover, D'Oyly, and I shall return. But there will be nothing to discuss.
(*Music cue 3 ends.*)

LUCY's *bedroom. Night.* LUCY (*hereafter called* KITTY *because that's Gilbert's nickname for her*) *is sitting up in bed in her nightdress. She is holding an open book.* GILBERT, *in evening wear, sits on an armchair. The bed is a four-poster with a canopy.*
KITTY: Did you dine at the Beefsteak Club?
GILBERT: Yes. Somewhat unsatisfactory.
KITTY: Oh? Well, you missed Mrs Judd's rabbit curry.
GILBERT: One gets the impression that everyone is snickering behind one's back.
KITTY: Perhaps you could have some for tomorrow's lunch.
GILBERT: 'The King of Topsy-Turvydom'. Humiliating.
(*Pause. Music cue 4 starts.*)
KITTY: You look a little uncomfortable.
GILBERT: I'm comfortable enough. I watched a bit from the wings.

KITTY: Oh, did you?
GILBERT: The first act. Seemed to be going rather well, surprisingly.
KITTY: There, you see. (*Pause.*) Would you like me to read to you?
GILBERT: No, thank you. I'll leave you. You must be tired.
(*He gets up, and stands at the foot of her bed.*)
KITTY: No, I'm not in the slightest.
GILBERT: It's wrong of me to unburden myself on you.
KITTY: Don't be silly. That's why I'm here. (*patting the eiderdown*) Come here and talk to your Kitty.
GILBERT: Sometimes one wonders why one bothers. They say 'jump', you jump. Goodnight, my dear.
(*He leaves, closing the door behind him.*)
KITTY: Goodnight.
(*She sits back, and reflects. Music cue 4 ends.*)

SULLIVAN's *apartment, his study. He is playing the* Piano Duet for Four Hands, Opus 10, *by Weber with a lady whose broad-brimmed hat makes her seem enigmatic. She is Sullivan's mistress,* MRS FANNY RONALDS.

A little later, in SULLIVAN's *drawing-room. He and* FANNY *are relaxing on an ottoman. The room is ornate and a touch exotic.*

SULLIVAN *is smoking the usual cigarette in its holder.* FANNY *takes this from him, and has a drag. She almost coughs, then gives it back to him. She has an American accent.*

FANNY: Lady Colin is endeavouring to persuade us to take up smoking. She's writing an article for the *Saturday Review*. She proposes that nicotine is a gift from the gods, and if men may benefit from its soothing qualities, why then may women not also? My poor daughter now believes that smoking is an extension of the communion between a woman and her husband.

SULLIVAN: Will she be smoking a cigarette on her wedding day?

FANNY (*laughing*): Heaven forfend!

(SULLIVAN *laughs*.)

Lady Colin is irresistible. She cannot conceive why the Irish are starving when there's lots of good fish in the sea.

SULLIVAN: She most probably has a point.

FANNY: Oh, there's good news from Dublin.

SULLIVAN: Mm?

FANNY: The Churchills *are* to return to London.

SULLIVAN: Forgiven, but not forgotten.
FANNY: I do hope so. (*She takes the cigarette.*) Jenny says Winston is eleven, covered in freckles, and has a total disdain for authority.
(*She takes a drag, and returns the cigarette to* SULLIVAN. *He takes her hand, and kisses it. Then he sniffs it delicately.*)
SULLIVAN: Mmm . . . I shall miss this fragrance.
FANNY: Sicilian lemons. Have you chosen your Beethoven for the Philharmonic Society?
SULLIVAN: As a matter of fact, I have, yes.
FANNY: Number Two?
SULLIVAN: The Seventh.
FANNY: Ah.
SULLIVAN: More dramatic.
FANNY: And that is to be your work whilst you're away?
SULLIVAN: That, and only that.
FANNY: Will there be room for Mr Gilbert in your baggage?
SULLIVAN: Certainly not. He's far too large.
FANNY: Food for thought. *Ce n'est pas à moi de dire.*
(*She takes off her neck-brooch, and starts to unbutton her blouse.*)
SULLIVAN: Indeed not.
FANNY: Which train will you catch?
SULLIVAN: The tidal train. (*Pause.*) Up at seven.
FANNY: *Arriver à Paris à trois heures et demi.*
SULLIVAN: *À peu près.*
FANNY: How will you spend your first night of liberty?
SULLIVAN: I shall take some exercise.
FANNY: Hm.
(*She pulls out a watch on a chain, opens the clasp and looks at the time.* SULLIVAN *is smiling to himself.* FANNY *gives him an intense look. He catches her eye, and becomes reciprocally intense.*)

A brothel in Paris. A room. Ornate. Lots of candles. A severe, foppish fellow plays an upright piano and sings 'Les Oiseaux dans la Charmille' (the Clockwork Doll song from Offenbach's Tales of Hoffmann) *in a shrill falsetto. On a tiny stage, two* PROSTITUTES, *one sitting on the other's knee, and both naked above the waist, perform a comic 'Clockwork Doll' dance routine; this includes the naughty pinching of nipples, and much laughter and whooping.*

SULLIVAN, *a cigarette in one hand and a glass of champagne in the other, sits with the* MADAME. *There are no other clients or prostitutes in the room.* SULLIVAN *is thoroughly enjoying the entertainment, and throws in the odd jolly comment in French, as does the* MADAME.
PIANIST (*singing*):
> Les oiseaux dans la charmille,
> Dans les cieux l'astre du jour,
> Tout parle à la jeune-fille,
> Tout parle à la jeune-fille
> D'amour!
> (*During the prolonged note of 'D'amour!' the women stand, and go into a slinky routine.* SULLIVAN *strokes the* MADAME's *neck.*)

FIRST PROSTITUTE: *Vous aimez ma cuisse?*
SULLIVAN: *Plus de cuisse!*
MADAME: *Et voilà, voilà!*
PIANIST (*sings*):
> Ah!
> tout parle d'amour!
> Ah! Voilà la chanson gentille . . .
> (*The dance has progressed to the can can style.* SULLIVAN *is much amused.*)

A little later. SULLIVAN *embraces the* FIRST PROSTITUTE.
SULLIVAN: *Comment vous appelez-vous?*
MADAME: *Voilà Mademoiselle Fromage, monsieur.*
MLLE FROMAGE: *Mademoiselle Fromage.*
SULLIVAN: *Non, c'est pas vrai!*
MLLE FROMAGE: *Oui, c'est vrai!*
> (*The* SECOND PROSTITUTE *strokes* SULLIVAN's *hair.*)
SULLIVAN: *Mademoiselle Fromage. Quelle sorte de fromage?*
> (*The* MADAME *laughs.* MADEMOISELLE FROMAGE *can't think of an answer.*)
> *Peut-être un fromage suisse, eh?*
MLLE FROMAGE: *Ah, oui, oui!*
SULLIVAN: *Avec des petits trous?*
> (MADEMOISELLE FROMAGE *pretends to be shocked. The other two women laugh.* SULLIVAN *kisses* MADEMOISELLE FROMAGE *between the breasts. She squeals. Then he kisses the other lady in the same place. More laughter.*)

The Savoy Theatre. A performance of Princess Ida. *The three* BROTHERS *in armour stand in a straight line, facing the audience. Behind them is a front-cloth depicting a castle wall, portcullis, etc. The actors are very hot, and are sweating profusely.* CELLIER, *also sweating, is conducting with great effort. The audience is sparse. The few women present fan themselves relentlessly.*

KITTY *is in a theatre box. She is also fanning herself. She peers through opera glasses at the stage. Then she surveys the meagre audience. The actor in the centre of the trio is* RICHARD TEMPLE.

TEMPLE (*sings*):
    This helmet, I suppose,
    Was meant to ward off blows.
    It's very hot,
    And weighs a lot,
    As many a guardsman knows,
    As many a guardsman knows;
    As many a guardsman knows,
    As many a guardsman knows,
    So off, so off that helmet goes.
    (*He removes his helmet, and gives it to an* ATTENDANT, *who backs off the stage with it. We hear, but do not see, the* CHORUS *of men and women.*)

CHORUS (*sings*):
    Yes, yes, yes,
    So off that helmet goes!
    (KITTY *fans herself more profusely. It is suffocatingly hot.*)

TEMPLE (*sings*):
    This tight-fitting cuirass
    (*He thumps his chest.*)
    Is but a useless mass.
    It's made of steel,
    And weighs a deal –
    This tight-fitting cuirass
    Is but a useless mass.
    A man is but an ass
    Who fights in a cuirass,
    So off, so off, goes that cuirass.
    (*He has removed one of his gauntlets in order to undo and take*

off his cuirass (breastplate). Again, the ATTENDANT *takes this, and backs off the stage.)*

CHORUS (*sings*):
Yes, yes, yes,
So off goes that cuirass!

TEMPLE *is at his dressing-room mirror. During the following, he pulls off his bald wig and his crêpe moustache and beard, and removes his grease-paint with cream.*

TEMPLE: Behold! My voice . . . my voice – I've . . . strained my voice. I've been trying too hard. The smaller the house, the greater the effort. I'm very cross with myself. I should know better. One's knocking one's pipes out in a vain attempt to elicit a response from three colonial bishops, two elderly ladies and an intoxicated costermonger. And they're all roasting in their own lard like the Christmas goose!
(*The camera has pulled back to reveal that another actor shares this dressing-room. This is* DURWARD LELY. *He is standing, smoking a cigarette and gazing at himself in his mirror, whilst his* DRESSER (BUTT), *behind him, laces up his corset.* BUTT, *whom we saw earlier, wears a bowler hat.*)

LELY (*Scots accent*): Yes, and the costermonger left at the interval.

TEMPLE: Did he?

LELY: Mm.

TEMPLE: Ha! A man of infinite taste. Clearly.

LELY: Will you take a wee gargle of my salt water, Dickie?

TEMPLE: Oh, no thank you, dear chap. It would put me in mind of my boyhood.

LELY: Do forgive me.

TEMPLE: Not at all. (*Pause.*) I fear that dear Mr Gilbert has run out of ideas.

LELY: No!

TEMPLE: He doesn't know what to do with me. Ponder this: he thrusts me into a gamut of tight-fitting pots, pans and pails, and poaches me like a fucking haddock. Forgive my Anglo-Saxon, Mr Butt – do have a biscuit.

BUTT (*Northern*): Oh, thank you, sir. I'll take one 'ome with me for me supper.

LELY: Dickie, it's just this heat. It addles the noodles. It happened to me in Milan frequently.

TEMPLE: Ah, *Milano bellissimo*! The heat less hellish. I am humiliated. One might as well be in the chorus.

LELY: Och – away wi' you, you wee monkey!

TEMPLE: Alas, no. The reign of the Emperor Gilbert is all but at an end.

LELY (*turning round*): I consider this to be his best piece so far.

TEMPLE: With all due respect, my dear Durward, your romantic opinion may be informed by the fact that you take a rather good role, in which, of course, you are *très splendide*.

LELY: Mmm – *grazie*.

TEMPLE: *Prego*. But I consider *Princess Ida* to be their worst.

LELY: Do you?

TEMPLE: I do. Where is the panache of *Pirates*? The wit of the *Pinafore*? (*He goes into a West Country accent – Dick Deadeye in* HMS Pinafore) 'From such a face and form as mine, the noblest sentiments sound like the black utterances of a depraved imagination . . .' It was very good, you know!

LELY: Yes, Dickie.

TEMPLE: Do forgive me, dear boy. I don't wish to be the prophet of doom, but one cannot help but have the distinct feeling that the Sword of Damocles hovers ominously over the Savoy Theatre. (*He wipes his eye make-up.*)

GILBERT *and* KITTY *take breakfast. They sit at each end of the long table. Shelves laden with blue-and-white pottery behind them. They are eating solid fare with knives and forks.* GILBERT *is dressed, but without his jacket.* KITTY *is in normal day wear.*

GILBERT: How was Temple?

KITTY: Oh! Rather disgruntled, I fear. As though he wasn't quite enjoying himself.

GILBERT: His heart wasn't in it.

KITTY: No. One can usually rely on Mr Temple, can't one?

GILBERT: Mm.

KITTY: And the ladies' chorus look as though they could all do with a hearty meal.

GILBERT: This infernal heat.

KITTY: One still has to feed oneself, Willie, whatever the weather.

GILBERT: Mm.

KITTY: And the audience were fanning themselves with their programmes and libretti. Most distracting, when one is striving to concentrate on the performance, to have in the corner of one's eye this confounded flapping. It makes one want to stand up and shout.

GILBERT: I trust you restrained yourself.

KITTY: Yes, of course I did, Willie.

(PIDGEON, *the butler, comes in.*)

PIDGEON: More tea, ma'am?

KITTY: No, thank you, Pidgeon.

PIDGEON: Coffee, sir?

GILBERT: Yes. Pidgeon.

(PIDGEON *picks up* GILBERT*'s cup and saucer.*)

PIDGEON: Sir?

GILBERT: Did my father say anything else?

PIDGEON: Nothing I should care to repeat, sir. (PIDGEON *goes to the sideboard.*)

KITTY: There were more people on the stage than in the audience.

GILBERT: Did you count them? (*Short pause.*)

KITTY: No, of course I didn't, Willie.

GILBERT: Then how do you know?

KITTY: I was speaking metaphorically.

GILBERT: You were exaggerating.

(PIDGEON *gives* GILBERT *his coffee.*)

PIDGEON: Anything else, sir?

GILBERT: No, thank you.

PIDGEON: Ma'am. (PIDGEON *heads for the door.*)

GILBERT: 'Oh, horror! Horror! Horror!!'

(PIDGEON *turns and looks at* GILBERT. *Then he leaves.*)

KITTY: Willie!

HELEN*'s office at the Savoy. She is pouring coffee. A man, visible through a frosted glass-panelled door, knocks.*

HELEN: Come in.

(*He comes in. He is* RICHARD BARKER, *Carte's company*

manager. *He wears spectacles and a beard, and is dressed in full top hat and coat. He does not take off his hat. He carries a cane and some sheets of paper.*)

BARKER: Good morning, my dear.

HELEN: Good morning, Richard.

(BARKER *closes the door, and passes through the room.*)

Another scorcher.

BARKER: The everlasting bonfire. Good morning, guv'nor.

CARTE: Morning, Barker.

(CARTE, *in his shirtsleeves, sits behind his desk in the adjacent office.* BARKER *taps on the door frame with his cane, goes straight in, and gives* CARTE *the papers.*)

Thank you. (*Brief glance.*) Shocking!

BARKER: Most alarming. A mediocre evening. Three fainters.

(HELEN *brings in a tray of coffee, which she dispenses.*)

HELEN: In the audience?

BARKER: I fear so. All women.

HELEN: Any absentees?

CARTE: Four chorus members.

HELEN: With doctors' notes?

CARTE: Yes. (*Coffee.*) Thank you.

HELEN: And how are the returns?

(CARTE *shows her the sheet.*)

Oh, good grief.

CARTE: It's an improvement on Monday.

(CARTE *opens his cigarette box for* BARKER, *who takes one, and sits down on an ottoman.*)

BARKER: Seven dead horses in the Strand this morning – well . . . one down by Trafalgar Square.

CARTE: I don't know how you can sit there in your hat and coat, Barker.

(BARKER *lights his cigarette.*)

BARKER: I'm too hot to remove them, Mr Carte.

CARTE: This is developing into something of a crisis.

BARKER: Indeed it is. A man has a wife and children to support.

HELEN: I fear we shall all have to pray for rain.

BARKER: Well, if it's any consolation, every theatre in town is afflicted. Even the Gaiety, graced as it is with Madame

Bernhardt's execrable Lady Macbeth – thirty-eight per cent.
CARTE: Who told you that, Barker?
BARKER: Hollingshead. I, er – played a game of cricket with him this morning before breakfast at Coram's Fields.
HELEN: In this heat?
BARKER: Er, yes, madame, but not in this attire.
HELEN: Oh, good.
CARTE: Mr Hollingshead has told you a fib, Barker.
BARKER: Indeed?
CARTE: He's only playing to twenty-nine per cent.
(BARKER *presses an electric bell on the telephone, and stands up.*)
BARKER: Mr Hollingshead has no need to lie to me, Mr Carte.
CARTE: Mr Hollingshead has much need to lie to everybody, Mr Barker. Especially you.
HELEN: Gentlemen!
(*She gives* CARTE *an amused look, and returns to her office. Pause.* BARKER *leans on* CARTE's *chair. The telephone rings.* BARKER *leaps forward, picks up the earpiece, and shouts down the mouthpiece.*)
BARKER: Are you there? (*Pause.*) Yes. 8–5–0–5.

GILBERT, *in his study. He walks briskly over to a sort of telephone booth, opens the doors, turns on an electric light and picks up the receiver. The following conversation is shouted. We cut variously between the two talkers.*
GILBERT: Hello?
BARKER: Is that you, Mr Gilbert?
GILBERT: Hello?
BARKER: Hello?
GILBERT: Good morning, Barker.
BARKER: This is Barker speaking.
GILBERT: Gilbert here.
BARKER: Good morning, Mr Gilbert!
(KITTY *is standing, listening. She is holding a blue cushion. With her is a very* OLD MAN (DR WILLIAM GILBERT, *Gilbert's father) with long white side-whiskers.*)
GILBERT: How are we today, Barker? Are we popular or are we mad?

(BARKER *consults a white card in his hand.*)
BARKER: Er . . . er, we are popular.
GILBERT: Very good. Carry on.
(CARTE *holds up the returns for* BARKER *to see.*)
BARKER: Here is your message for today . . . (*He checks the returns and the card.*) 'U', 'U', plus ten shillings and sixpence.
(*A close-up of the card. It reads:*)

FAVOURITES
1 2 3 4 5 6 7 8 9 0

HYSTERICAL
1 2 3 4 5 6 7 8 9 0

GILBERT: Can you repeat that, please?
BARKER: Yes. 'U' . . . 'U'.
GILBERT: So that's 'U' for 'udder' –?
BARKER: Yes.
GILBERT: 'U' for udder –?
BARKER: Yes.
GILBERT: Plus ten shillings and sixpence.
BARKER: Yes.
(GILBERT *writes down this information.* DR GILBERT *gives* KITTY *a bewildered look. She lowers her eyes.*)
GILBERT: So you have two, udders, Barker?
BARKER: Er, yes.
GILBERT: I always suspected as much.
(BARKER *guffaws uproariously.* CARTE *remains impassive.*)
Thank you.
BARKER: Thank you.
GILBERT: Goodbye.
BARKER: Goodbye, Mr Gilbert. (*He almost hangs up the receiver, but –*)
GILBERT: I'm going to hang up the telephone now.
BARKER: Indeed you are, sir.
(BARKER *hangs up his earpiece, and presses the bell on the telephone. Music cue 5 starts.* GILBERT *hangs up.*)
Well, I'm er . . . going out to seek a little Italian hokey-pokey, and I care not who knows it.

CARTE (*without looking up*): Thank you, Barker.
(BARKER *opens the door, and turns to* CARTE.)
BARKER: I shall not return with any for you, sir, because it would melt. *Au revoir.*
(*He closes the door behind him.* CARTE *is entirely preoccupied with his sums.*)

Meanwhile, back in GILBERT*'s large, bright, oak-panelled study with its huge fireplace, its well-stocked bookshelves and its bric-à-brac.* GILBERT *crosses to the desk, which is in a bay window.*

GILBERT: I owe you an apology, Kitty. It would appear you weren't exaggerating after all.
KITTY: Apology accepted – thank you, Willie. (*To* DR GILBERT:) Schwenck speaks to the Savoy every morning in code, father-in-law, just in case the telephone operator should be eavesdropping.
DR GILBERT: One might as well open the window and shout down the street.
(KITTY *places the cushion on the sofa.*)
KITTY: There, that should be more comfortable for you.
DR GILBERT: Sheer waste of time. It can only result in the further erosion of the written word.
KITTY (*indicating sofa*): Would you care to sit down now?
DR GILBERT: Thank ye. (*But he sits on an armchair.*)
(PIDGEON *comes in, and collects cups and saucers.*)
KITTY: Ah, there you are, Pidgeon.
PIDGEON: Ma'am.
(*Music cue 5 ends.* KITTY *sits by* DR GILBERT. GILBERT *himself checks the coded message, and enters the information in a large ledger.*)
KITTY: I do apologize, sir, that neither I nor Schwenck was here to welcome you on your arrival last night.
DR GILBERT: I do not appreciate being left upon the doorstep like a hawker!
GILBERT: If you'll only take the trouble to press the electric bell, Father, you'll be admitted at once. Is that not so, Pidgeon?
PIDGEON: Indeed it is, sir.
DR GILBERT: I have no intention of placing my life in danger, sir!

GILBERT: How many doorstep deaths have we had thus far, Pidgeon?
PIDGEON: Er, none to my certain knowledge, sir.
GILBERT: There you are, Father. The odds would appear to be in your favour.
(PIDGEON *picks up the tray.*)
PIDGEON: Will there be anything else, sir?
GILBERT: No, thank you.
KITTY: Would you tell Mrs Judd that Dr Gilbert will be joining us for lunch?
PIDGEON: Certainly, ma'am. (PIDGEON *goes.*)
KITTY: You know, Father-in-law, that you are most welcome in our home at any time; but please do try to inform us of your intention to visit.
DR GILBERT: A father should not have to seek permission to visit his own son.
GILBERT: The son shouldn't be expected to be clairvoyant.
DR GILBERT: Who does he think I am? Harlequin?
KITTY: Would you excuse me?
(*She gets up. They do so, too.*)
I take it that you will be joining us for lunch, Father-in-law?
DR GILBERT: I – I have no idea where I shall be taking luncheon, thank ye.
KITTY: Well, perhaps Schwenck can persuade you.
(*She leaves.* GILBERT *closes the doors of the telephone booth.*)
GILBERT: Take lunch with us, Father. We shall enjoy your company.

Moments later. GILBERT *is back at his desk.* DR GILBERT *is still standing.*
DR GILBERT: Am I to understand, sir, that you have been in communication with your mother?
GILBERT: No, Father, not for some considerable time, I'm glad to say.
DR GILBERT: You are a liar, sir.
(GILBERT *gets up and turns to face his father.*)
GILBERT: No, sir. I can assure you, Papa, that the very last person with whom I wish to have any communication at all

is your estranged wife . . . the vicious woman who bore me into this ridiculous world.

DR GILBERT: How dare you, sir? Have you no respect?!

GILBERT: Don't misunderstand me, Father: nobody respects her more than I do, and I can't stand the woman.

DR GILBERT: She is a veritable gorgon.

GILBERT: She is indeed, and she has chosen her own path, and in so doing, she has turned her back on yourself and myself. And for that small mercy we should both of us be eternally grateful.

(GILBERT *returns to his desk and his work.* DR GILBERT *sits on the sofa. He looks about him, fearfully.*)

DR GILBERT: Those terrors . . . that visit me . . . in the night . . . They can never be vanquished!

GILBERT: Ah, insomnia. I suffer from it myself.

DR GILBERT: But it is she who sends them. I know it is she.

(GILBERT *turns round and looks at his father in surprise.*)

I know not what heathen oracles she consults, what filthy familiar she employs, but I know that . . . they will come . . . Wh-wh-what are these walls?

(*Whatever 'these walls' are, they apparently close in on* DR GILBERT, *gradually at first, then rapidly. He is very frightened and disturbed. He moans and groans and shrieks, and, finally, screams with terror, shielding his eyes from the awful spectre. Then the crisis appears to subside. But not the fit:* DR GILBERT *is now very much in another reality. He is still experiencing something very unsettling. His hands flutter about his face involuntarily.* GILBERT *watches all this in horror, disgust and sadness. Finally, he looks away.*)

A bustling Paris restaurant. (*Music cue 6 starts.*) CARTE *and* SULLIVAN *have a table by the wall.* SULLIVAN *is reading a document.* CARTE *watches him.*

SULLIVAN: Five thousand pounds!

CARTE: The last ten shares – worth every penny. Trust me, Arthur. (CARTE *holds out an object resembling a fountain pen.*)

SULLIVAN: I do, D'Oyly. What's this? (*He takes it.*)

CARTE: Pull it.
(*He gestures; bemused,* SULLIVAN *pulls off the top.*)
SULLIVAN: Oh!
CARTE: It's a reservoir pen. Contains its own ink.
SULLIVAN: Good gracious me. Whatever will they think of next?
CARTE: Try it.
(SULLIVAN *cautiously writes his signature.*)
SULLIVAN: Ha! (*Pause.*) Now . . . how long is all this going to take?
CARTE: Two years. I shall begin the foundations next month. Thank you.
(SULLIVAN *has returned the pen and the document. He takes his monocle out of his eye, and raises his champagne glass.*)
SULLIVAN: To the Savoy Hotel!
CARTE: The Savoy Hotel!
(*They clink glasses.*)
SULLIVAN: With its seventy bathrooms.
(*They drink.* CARTE *puts the document in his briefcase.*)
CARTE: The builder was much bemused. (*Cockney accent.*) 'What's the point of 'avin' a bathroom to every bedroom? 'Oo's goin' to be stayin' there? Amphibians?'
SULLIVAN: D'Oyly, I can't tell you how delightful it is to see you here in Paris.
CARTE: You're looking much better.
SULLIVAN: A new man. Monte Carlo was most profitable. Florence was hideously hot. I sampled the Chartreuse at Certoza. The monks were uncommonly charming. The train journey through the St Gothard Pass is spectacular – you must go. And Lucerne . . . tranquillity itself. I walked until I dropped.
CARTE: Did you receive my letter?
(*Pause.*)
SULLIVAN: Yes, I did.
(*Pause.*)
CARTE: Good. And?
SULLIVAN: It came to Brussels.
CARTE: I sent it to Brussels, Arthur.
SULLIVAN: Yes, of course.

(SULLIVAN *has taken out a cigarette, and is about to fix it into his holder. The* WAITER *arrives with the bread.*)
CARTE: *Nous sommes prêts.*
(SULLIVAN *puts the cigarette away.* CARTE *watches him. The* WAITER *serves their meals.*)
SULLIVAN: *Vous avez tué ce pigeon, vous-même?*
WAITER (*dour*): *Non, monsieur – je laisse au bourreau le soin de le faire.*
SULLIVAN: *C'est mieux comme ça.*
WAITER: *Monsieur.* (*He removes the empty champagne glasses.*)
CARTE: So, what is your position?
(*Pause.* SULLIVAN *sighs. The* WAITER *pours their wine.*)
SULLIVAN: Much the same, I'm afraid. I fully realize, D'Oyly, that you have me under contract. But I cannot write any more operas for the Savoy. (*Pause.*) At least, not of that particular character.
CARTE: I think you should tell Gilbert.
SULLIVAN: I shall . . . The minute I return.
(*Music cue 6 ends.*)
WAITER: *Messieurs, je vous souhait un bon appétit.*
CARTE: *Merci.*
SULLIVAN: *Merci.*
(*Silence. They tackle the pigeon.*)

SULLIVAN's *London apartment, the study. Afternoon.* SULLIVAN *is at the piano.* FANNY *stands beside him, wearing her hat and gloves. She is singing* (*her own 'Barcarole', words by Edgar Berry*).
FANNY (*sings*):
    The reason is not far to find
    When we are near,
    For though they say that love is blind,
    Ah, never fear.
    Ah! Ah! Ah!
SULLIVAN (*joining in*):
    Ah! Ah! Ah!
FANNY (*solo*):
    We see our destinies entwined
    In noon-day clear,
    And love is overall

When shadows fall
And thou art here.
(SULLIVAN *concludes his accompaniment with a flourish as* FANNY *moves to the sofa, and stands with her back to it.* SULLIVAN *takes out his monocle and laughs heartily.* FANNY *falls backwards over the sofa, and* SULLIVAN *dives on top of her. He chortles, she squeals, and they both roll about gleefully.*)

A little later. SULLIVAN*'s reception lobby.* FANNY *briskly follows* CLOTHILDE, *putting on her gloves as she goes.*
FANNY: *Il est bien, Clothilde.*
CLOTHILDE: Oui, madam, you are a tonic for 'im.
FANNY: *Merci.* Cherish him.
(*She touches* CLOTHILDE*'s arm.*)
CLOTHILDE: Of course, madam.
(CLOTHILDE *opens the front door. Coincidentally* GILBERT *arrives at this moment. This makes* CLOTHILDE *jump, and she takes a few moments to get over it.*)
GILBERT: Ah, Mrs Ronalds, what an unexpected pleasure! (*He takes off his hat.*)
FANNY: Mr Gilbert, how are you?
GILBERT: How are you?
FANNY: Quite well, thank you.
GILBERT: I'm so pleased.
FANNY: He's in excellent spirits.
GILBERT: Is he? I look forward to hearing his tales.
FANNY: Good day.
GILBERT: Good day to you.
FANNY (*to* CLOTHILDE): *Au revoir.*
CLOTHILDE: *Madame.*
(FANNY *leaves.* CLOTHILDE *closes the door behind her.* GILBERT *gives her his hat, cane and gloves.*)
GILBERT: *Ça va*, Clothilde?
CLOTHILDE: *Ça va, monsieur.* It is 'ot, no?
GILBERT: Yes.
CLOTHILDE: 'E awaits.
GILBERT: Thank you.
(GILBERT *goes one way,* CLOTHILDE *the other.*)

A few minutes later in SULLIVAN*'s study.* GILBERT *and* SULLIVAN *are sitting side by side on the sofa. A large tray full of silver coffeeware and cups and saucers sits in front of them on a low table.*
GILBERT: How was your crossing, Sullivan?
SULLIVAN: Mercifully smooth, thank you.
GILBERT: As smooth as D'Oyly Carte!
(*They laugh uproariously.*)
SULLIVAN: No, not quite, Gilbert.
(*He picks up a silver sugar bowl and offers it to* GILBERT.)
Lump sugar?
GILBERT: Thank you, no.
SULLIVAN: Oh, please – do. I found it in Lucerne. It's delicious.
GILBERT (*chuckling*): If you insist.
(*He takes one, and pops it in his mouth.* SULLIVAN *does the same.*)
Mmm – very good.
(SULLIVAN *puts the bowl back on the tray. They talk for a little while with their mouths full.*)
SULLIVAN: Is Lucy well?
GILBERT: Oh, she's in fine fettle. She sends you her love, and trusts you are in good health.

SULLIVAN: Thank you. Please reciprocate.
GILBERT: Oh, of course. Now, what's this Carte's been telling me?
SULLIVAN: Oh, dear.
GILBERT: You can't be serious.
SULLIVAN: I'm afraid I am.
GILBERT (*jovial*): So you've torn up our contract into tiny pieces, and cast it to the four winds!
SULLIVAN: Oh, don't be absurd.
GILBERT: That would be the implication.
SULLIVAN: I hardly think so.
GILBERT: What else is one to deduce?
SULLIVAN: Oh, Gilbert . . . There's so much that I have yet to do for music, for my queen, for my country. Even if God were to grant me two days for every one that I have left on this earth, I still should not be able to achieve everything.
GILBERT: Come, come, Sullivan – you're a genius. I merely bask in your reflected glory.
SULLIVAN (*laughing coyly*): Oh, Gilbert, please.
GILBERT: But I am somewhat at a loss. What is the precise nature of your dilemma?
SULLIVAN: How shall I put this? (*Pause.*) My tunes . . . my – my orchestrations are becoming repetitive. I've rung all the changes possible in the way of variety of rhythm. I have such respect for your words that I have continually kept down my music in order that they can be heard. It's no more than word-setting.
GILBERT: Sullivan, I – I have always subordinated my words to your music.
SULLIVAN: Oh, I think not.
GILBERT: You've often expatiated to me and to others on the thorough good feeling with which we've always worked together.
SULLIVAN: Unquestionably. But I want a chance for my music to act in its own proper sphere.
GILBERT: It does. It always has, and it always will.
SULLIVAN: It must be allowed to intensify the emotional element – not only of your words, but of the situation, which can be humorous, dramatic – what you will.

GILBERT: Of course. It goes without saying – you teach me the ABC of my profession. Now, would you care for me to read this to you or not? (*He takes out a large bound notebook, which he opens.*)

SULLIVAN (*unenthusiastically*): Where's it set?

GILBERT: In the Sicilian mountains. Plenty of scope there for gypsy music, one might suggest. Now the local alchemist is killed in an explosion, and there, amongst his effects, a chorus of villagers discover a potion.

SULLIVAN: A magic potion, no doubt.

GILBERT: Indeed.

SULLIVAN: Mm, I thought as much.

GILBERT: Now the effect of this magic potion is to transform the character who takes it into whatever he or she is pretending to be.

SULLIVAN: Oh, Gilbert! You and your world of topsy-turvydom. (GILBERT *laughs.*)
In 1881, it was a magic coin; and before that it was a magic lozenge; and in 1877 it was an elixir.

GILBERT: In this instance it is a magic potion. (*Reads:*) 'Act One. Scene: A mountain inn on a picturesque Sicilian pass. A range of mountains with Etna in the distance.'
(SULLIVAN *does not look happy.*)

Night. GILBERT *is in his study, working at the desk. His head is wrapped in a bandage. His housekeeper,* MRS JUDD, *comes in. She carries a tray.* (*Music cue 7 starts.*)

MRS JUDD (*Northern accent*): I've made you some beef tea, Mr Gilbert.

GILBERT: Take it away.

MRS JUDD: You've not had anything since yesterday afternoon, sir. (*She puts the tray on the desk.*)

GILBERT: Take it away.

MRS JUDD: You can't work on an empty stomach.

GILBERT: I can't work at all, Mrs Judd, if I'm being constantly pestered by interfering women with hot beef tea, cold compresses, mustard poultices and excessive attacks of philanthropic zeal.
(KITTY *has come in. She joins them.*)

KITTY: How's my wounded soldier?
MRS JUDD: He's not doing as he's told, madam.
KITTY: Oh, isn't he, now? Willie, are you intending to visit the dentist tomorrow?
MRS JUDD: You really should try –
GILBERT (*shouting*): Oh, for God's sake, you pair of bloody harpies!! Get out! I'm working!
(MRS JUDD *leaves.* KITTY *moves to his other side. She touches his shoulder gently.*)
KITTY: Willie –
GILBERT: Madam, I had rather spend an afternoon in a Turkish bath with my mother than visit the dratted dentist.
KITTY: Very well. Goodnight.
(*She walks towards the door. The Housemaid arrives with a jug, but a glance from* KITTY *persuades her to leave immediately.* KITTY *goes out.* GILBERT *continues writing. Then he stops to ponder.*)

Next day. GILBERT *sits in the* DENTIST'*s chair. The* DENTIST *holds his head in a tight grip. He is removing the offending tooth with forceps.*

GILBERT (*screaming*): Aaargh!!!
DENTIST: She's being just a little bit tricky.
GILBERT: Aaargh! Aaargh! Aargh!
DENTIST: She's coming . . .
GILBERT: Aah – Aah – Aah – Aaah!!!
(*The tooth comes out.* GILBERT *gasps and groans. Music cue 7 ends.*)
DENTIST: Well done, Mr Gilbert. (*He gives* GILBERT *a glass of water.*) Rinse. She's a beauty.
(GILBERT *rinses his mouth. The* DENTIST *removes the glass.*)
Open wide.
(*He puts a swab in* GILBERT*'s mouth.*)
Bite, really hard.
(GILBERT *groans.*)
I must say, my wife and I did find *Princess Ida* rather too long, don't you know.
(GILBERT *tries to say something.*)
Try not to speak, old chap.
(*He wipes his hands.* GILBERT *looks helpless.*)

A large, fashionable room in a house. Late afternoon. A young man is playing a grand piano for an audience of some twenty or so ladies and gentlemen who are arranged in rows on chairs. (*He is playing* Nocturne No. 4 in E Flat Major, Opus 36 *by Fauré.*)

SULLIVAN *enters discreetly, his door opened by a Footman. He looks round. Then he tiptoes over to* FANNY, *who is at the back of the audience, leaning on an ornate sideboard. They exchange glances, and she takes his hand for a few moments. They listen to the music. It comes to an end. Everybody claps, and* FANNY *moves away from* SULLIVAN.

A short time later. FANNY *appears in front of the audience, holding a piece of sheet music. Applause. She is obviously the hostess. This is her 'salon'. In fact, it is her house. She raises her hands slightly, a modest request for the applause to cease. The audience obliges.*
FANNY: I do hope you've enjoyed your evening, but . . . before we say farewell, may I suggest an impromptu?
(*The audience murmurs enthusiastically.*)

Mr Walter Simmonds has generously offered to
accompany me on the harmonium!
(*Applause.* MR SIMMONDS *appears. He is the youth who
played the Fauré. He takes his place at the harmonium, which
is next to the piano.*)
Now . . . we have another very young hopeful with us this
evening, who has kindly agreed to accompany us with a
new composition of his own . . . 'The Lost Chord'!!
(*She holds up and reveals the song sheet. Much amusement and
enthusiastic applause, as* SULLIVAN *enters, beaming and
bowing.* FANNY *places the music on the piano.*)
Sir Arthur informed me a few moments ago that he cannot
entirely recall his new piece.
(*Laughter.*)

SULLIVAN (*very quietly*): *Merci, madame.*
(FANNY *directs another young man to the harmonium to turn
pages for* SIMMONDS. *Then she poses in profile between the two
instruments.* SULLIVAN *begins the introduction, accompanied
by* SIMMONDS. *'The Lost Chord' by Sullivan. Words by
Adelaide A. Procter.* FANNY *sings – as much for* SULLIVAN *as
for the audience.*)

FANNY (*sings*):
>   Seated one day at the organ,
>   I was weary and ill at ease,
>   And my fingers wandered idly
>   Over the noisy keys;
>   I know not what I was playing,
>   Or what I was dreaming then,
>   But I struck one chord of music
>   Like the sound of a great Amen.
>   Like the sound of a great Amen.

In CARTE*'s office.* CARTE *is at his desk.* GILBERT *is pacing about.*
CARTE: It's ridiculous.
GILBERT: It is. I sent him the thing on Monday of last week – he could've read it on the same day, or at the very least on Tuesday. Now ten days have passed, and I haven't heard a word.
CARTE: This concerns me greatly.
GILBERT: It concerns me greatly.
CARTE: You're going to have to go and see him, you know.
GILBERT: I'll be buggered if I do any such thing. I present the man with my idea, he rejects it, I respond in detail to his misgivings, but answer came there none. Now either he hasn't read it, or he has read it, and he doesn't like it. And if he doesn't like it he should say so. Then at least we shall know where we stand.
CARTE: Go and see him.
GILBERT: No, Carte – you go and see him. I have no more shots in my locker.
(*He inspects a framed poster on Carte's wall:* HMS Pinafore, Or The Lass That Loved A Sailor, *by Sullivan and Gilbert.*) Sullivan and Gilbert – who are they? At least we're finally going to revive *The Sorcerer*.
CARTE: Only as a stop-gap.
GILBERT: It'll give us breathing space.
CARTE: It won't run more than three months.
GILBERT: Your unbounded optimism is inspiring, Carte.
CARTE: I have the greatest confidence in *The Sorcerer*, Gilbert, but I'm not in the business of revivals.

GILBERT: You are now, since you've decided to withdraw the ailing *Princess Ida*, in spite of the cooler weather.

A performance of The Sorcerer *at the Savoy Theatre. The Incantation Scene from Act 1. The setting: outside a mansion, with misty meadows beyond. Moving cloud effects on the back-cloth. Darkness. On stage are* GEORGE GROSSMITH, DURWARD LELY *and the leading soprano* LEONORA BRAHAM. GROSSMITH *is playing John Wellington Wells, the Sorcerer, stove-pipe top hat, sinister black suit and curly mutton chops;* LEONORA *is Aline, in her bridal frock; and* LELY *is Alexis, in a bright red military uniform. A table, laid for a banquet and decorated with flowers, stands centre stage.* CELLIER *is conducting the orchestra. There is a full house.*

Musical Introduction. GROSSMITH *prances round the stage, Victorian Grand Guignol style.* LEONORA *and* LELY *stand close together, holding hands, to one side of the stage. The lighting on the table turns to a red glow.* GROSSMITH *prances behind the table, and waves his hands about, as though casting a spell.*

GROSSMITH (*sings*):
    Sprites of earth and air –
    Fiends of flame and fire –
    Demon souls,
    Come here in shoals,
    This dreadful deed inspire!
    Appear, appear, appear!
    (*Backstage, in the wings. The stage manager signals to a man in a bowler hat and shirtsleeves, who operates a thunder-sheet vigorously. Lightning effects onstage. The male chorus is offstage. All are dressed as villagers, peasants and yokels. One of them, in a smock, conducts the rest as they sing.*)

MEN (*sing*):
    Good master, we are here!
    (GROSSMITH *moves downstage, striking a series of melodramatic 'attitudes'.*)

GROSSMITH (*sings*):
    Noisome hags of night –
    (*We see the piccolo player play five notes.*)
    Imps of deadly shade –
    Pallid ghosts.

Arise in hosts,
And lend me all your aid.
Appear, appear, appear!
(*A burst from the strings, a blast from the horns. Offstage, the ladies' chorus, located apart from the men, sings. They are conducted by one of their number, who is dressed as a rural wench. They are all villagers, yokels, etc.*)

LADIES (*sing*):
Good master, we are here!
(GROSSMITH *prances into the wings, bearing the teapot aloft. A stage-hand takes it, and the stage manager gives* GROSSMITH *something which he places in his inside pocket. Meanwhile,* LEONORA *and* LELY *sing.*)

LELY (*sings*):
Hark, hark, they assemble,
These fiends of the night!

LEONORA (*sings*):
Oh, Alexis, I tremble,
Seek safety in flight!
(CELLIER *conducts a vigorous burst of music.*)
Let us fly to a far-off land,
Where peace and plenty dwell –
Where the sigh of the silver strand
Is echoed in every shell.
To the joy that land will give,
On the wings of Love we'll fly;
In innocence there to live –
In innocence there to die!
In innocence there to live,
There to die, to live and die.
(*During* LEONORA*'s aria above, the ladies' chorus leader mimes in unison with her, obviously in the grip of a star-struck fantasy. She is overcome with emotion. The fellow-chorister beside her is plainly embarrassed, and another mimics her mockingly behind her back.*

Meanwhile, GROSSMITH *fans himself while he waits to go on.*

Then he does so, shuffling like a railway engine. He carries a duplicate teapot, to which is attached an electric cable.)

CHORUS (*sings*):
> To late! Too late!

GROSSMITH, LELY, LEONORA (*sing*):
> Too late! Too late!

CHORUS (*sings*):
> That may not be!

PRINCIPALS (*sing*):
> It may not be!

CHORUS (*sings*):
> That happy fate
> Is not for thee!

PRINCIPALS (*sing*):
> That happy fate
> Is not for thee!
>
> (GROSSMITH *puts the teapot on the table and comes downstage.*)

GROSSMITH (*sings*):
> Now, shrivelled hags, with poison bags,
> Discharge your loathsome loads!
> Spit flame and fire, unholy choir!
> Belch forth your venom, toads!
> Ye demons fell, with yelp and yell,
> Shed curses far afield –
> Ye fiends of night, your filthy blight
> In noisome plenty yield!
>
> (*In the wings, the stage-manager holds up his hand. His assistant holds a live wire to an electric detonator.* GROSSMITH *goes back behind the table, takes a phial from his inside pocket, and 'pours' it – stylized, magical – into the teapot.*)
>
> Number One!
>
> (*Sign from the stage-manager, assistant detonates – magic flash from the teapot.*)

CHORUS (*sings*):
> It is done!
>
> (GROSSMITH *takes out another phial. The technical business is repeated.*)

GROSSMITH (*sings*):
> Number Two!
> (*A flash.*)

CHORUS (*sings*):
>One too few!
>(*Same business again.*)

GROSSMITH (*sings*):
>Number Three!
>(*This time, not only does the teapot flash, but four explosions go off downstage, along the footlights, emitting four substantial puffs of smoke. Evocative music. Another burst from the thunder machine.* LEONORA *and* LELY *look suitably frightened. A woman in the stalls lowers her opera glasses.*)

CHORUS (*sings*):
>Set us free!
>Set us free – our work is done.
>Ha! ha! ha!
>Ha! ha! ha! ha! ha! ha! ha!

LEONORA AND LELY (*sing*):
>Let us fly to a far-off land,
>Where peace and plenty dwell –

CHORUS (*sings*):
>Set us free!
>Set us free!

GROSSMITH (*sings*):
>Too late!
>Too late!

LEONORA AND LELY (*sing*):
>Where the sigh of the silver strand
>Is echoed in every shell.

CHORUS (*sings*):
>Set us free!
>Set us free!

GROSSMITH (*sings*):
>Too late!
>Too late!
>(*The following sung ensemble.*)

CHORUS (*sings*):
>Ha! ha! ha! ha! ha!
>Ha! ha! ha! ha! ha!

LEONORA AND LELY (*sing*):
>Let us fly!

GROSSMAN (*sings*):
    Too late!

During the Interval. LEONORA, *still in her bridal wear, is smoking a cigarette in her dressing-room. She is watching* JESSIE BOND, *with whom she shares.* JESSIE, *who is wearing a domestic servant's costume, is leafing through a handful of unopened letters, whilst their dresser* (EMILY), *massages her leg.*

LEONORA: How many today, Jessie?
JESSIE (*mock melodramatic*): Only nine, alas!
LEONORA (*mock melodramatic*): Oh, alas! (*Normal*) I have received none today. I am utterly neglected!
JESSIE: Have these, you poor soul!
LEONORA: I don't want your scraps, Jessie Bond.
    (*She picks up a glass of sherry, and takes a sip.* JESSIE *speaks to* EMILY.)
JESSIE: Too vigorous, Emily. Apply the bandage.
EMILY: Beg your pardon, Miss Bond. (*She bandages a severe varicose vein.*)
LEONORA: Shall I ever find anybody again?
JESSIE: Oh, don't be so gloomy, Leonora.
LEONORA: Sadly, I seem to appeal only to elderly gentlemen. Where are my young bucks and blades? *Quelle dommage*!
JESSIE: I've told you what you must do.
LEONORA (*sighing*): The last thing a girl wants after an evening's performance is to have to go and sing all night for London society. Idle ladies and their odious husbands.
JESSIE: One has to sing for one's supper.
LEONORA: It's damned exhausting. I detest it. (*She empties her glass.*)
JESSIE: Anyway, they're not all married, and some of them are rather cute and courteous.
LEONORA: You have them dangling on a leash, Jessie.
JESSIE: One must keep oneself amused, don't you know.
    (*Pause.* LEONORA *pours herself another sherry.*)
LEONORA: It's so terribly trying. I meet a gentleman; he invites me to supper; I mention my little . . . secret; and then he's off, quick smart. *C'est impossible!*
JESSIE: Well, you shouldn't reveal your little secret until he's

fallen hopelessly in love with you, and has asked you to marry him.

LEONORA: Oh, Jessie, for goodness' sake! 'By the by, *monsieur*, you do realize, do you not, that I have a little boy?' I couldn't possibly pretend that Stanton doesn't exist – no. No, he's my precious little bundle.

JESSIE: How's his toothache?

LEONORA: Earache. He suffers terribly, poor mite.

(*In the pit, the orchestra has begun to tune up for the second act.*)

EMILY: Would you like me to lace you up now, Miss Bond?

(*She refers to Jessie's boot.*)

JESSIE: Of course, Emily. Surely your Mr Barnes would be willing?

LEONORA: Mr Baker. Jessie, please! I do not intend to become a widow again before I am fifty.

(JESSIE *is pulling up her stocking.*)

JESSIE: No, neither do I . . .

A few minutes later. JESSIE *and* LEONORA *are warming up their voices.* JESSIE *is powdering her face.* LEONORA *is holding her sherry. They sing ('Long Years Ago, Fourteen Maybe' from* Patience, Act 1.)

JESSIE AND LEONORA (*sing*):
  No doubt! Yet, spite of all my/your* pains,
  The interesting fact remains –
  (*A knock on the door.* JESSIE *carries on singing.* LEONORA *stops for a moment.*)

LEONORA: Come in.

JESSIE AND LEONORA (*sing*):
  He was a *little* boy!
  (*The door opens. It is* SHRIMP, *the call-boy.*)
  He was a little *boy*!
  (SHRIMP *waits until they've finished.*)

SHRIMP: Five minutes, Miss Braham.

LEONORA: Thank you, Shrimp.

SHRIMP (*tipping his cap*): Pleasure, miss.

---

* JESSIE: my / LEONORA: your

(*He leaves.* JESSIE *applies her make-up – with a rabbit's foot brush.* LEONORA *finishes her sherry.*)

On stage. The Sorcerer, *Act 2. Moonlight. Gilbert's stage instruction: 'All the peasantry are discovered asleep on the ground.'*
GROSSMITH, LEONORA *and* LELY *stand in the middle of the sleeping mass.* GROSSMITH *holds a lantern.*

GROSSMITH (*sing*):
> But soft – they waken, one by one –
> The spell has worked – the deed is done!
> I would suggest that we retire
> While Love, the Housemaid, lights her kitchen fire!

ALL THREE (*sing*):
> While Love, the Housemaid, lights her kitchen fire!
> (*They all creep off stealthily. Gilbert's stage instruction: 'Exeunt* MR WELLS, ALEXIS *and* ALINE, *on tiptoe, as the villagers stretch their arms, yawn, rub their eyes, and sit up.' The mood of the music changes as the lights come up with a great surge until the scene is bathed in bright sunlight. The chorus sings in 'Mummerset' accents.*)

MEN (*sing*):
> Why, where be Oi, and what be Oi a doin',
> A sleepin' out, just when the dew du rise?

WOMEN (*sing*):
> Why, that's the very way your 'ealth to ruin,
> And don't seem quite respectable likewise.

MEN (*sing, staring at women*):
> Eh, that's you!
> Only think of that now!
> (*The men get up, followed by the women.*)

WOMEN (*sing, coyly*):
> What may you be at, now?
> Tell me, du!
> (*A pirouette, and each woman sits on a man's knee. No couple matches, e.g., an ancient man with a young girl, etc.*)

MEN (*sing, admiringly*):
> Eh, what a nose,
> And oh, what eyes, miss!

Lips like a rose,
And cheeks likewise, miss!
WOMEN (*sing*):
Oi'll tell you true,
Which I've never done, sir,
Oi loike you
As Oi never loiked none, sir!
(*They all rise, do another twirl, and end up facing the front.*)
ALL (*sing*):
Eh, but Oi du loike you!!

SULLIVAN *is in his study, late at night. He is in his shirtsleeves, working at the desk – writing* [*like many composers,* SULLIVAN *didn't compose at the piano*]. *He has a cigarette in its holder.*

He writes a couple of bars, stops, crosses something out, and lets his pen drop on to the page. He holds his head in his hands. He lets his monocle drop. Near by, Big Ben strikes the quarter. He looks helpless. He is not happy.

In CARTE*'s office. Day. Footsteps. Until* GILBERT *and* SULLIVAN *sit, we see only a close shot of the desk: hands, cigars, etc.*

GILBERT: Good morning, Carte.
CARTE: Good morning, Gilbert. Cigar? (*He offers the cigar box.*)
GILBERT: Thank you very much. (*He takes one.*)
SULLIVAN: Gilbert.
GILBERT: Sullivan. May I? (*He refers to Carte's cigar-cutter.*)
CARTE: Certainly.
SULLIVAN: Good morning, D'Oyly.
CARTE: Hello, Arthur.
GILBERT: Good morning, Miss Lenoir.
HELEN: Good morning, everybody.
SULLIVAN: Good day, Helen.
   (GILBERT *and* SULLIVAN *sit, side by side.* GILBERT *lights his cigar.* CARTE *sits on the ottoman by the wall.* HELEN *sits in* CARTE's *chair behind his desk.* CARTE *gives her a discreet nod.*)
HELEN: Now, gentlemen, we all know why we're here. We seem to have come to something of a standstill.
SULLIVAN: Indeed we have.
HELEN: Which, Arthur, is because . . .?
SULLIVAN: Oh. Because, Helen, I am unable to set the piece that Gilbert persists in presenting.
GILBERT: The piece I persist in presenting, Sullivan, is substantially altered each time, otherwise there'd be little point in my presenting it to you.
   (SULLIVAN *lights a cigarette.*)
SULLIVAN: With great respect, old chap, it is not substantially altered at all. You seem merely to have grafted on to the first act the tantalizing suggestion that we are to be in the realms of human emotion and probability, only to disappoint us by reverting to your familiar world of topsy-turvydom.
GILBERT: That which I have grafted on to Act One, Sullivan, has been specifically at your request. If you take exception to topsy-turvydom, you take exception to a great deal of my work over the past twenty-five years. Not to mention much of what you and I have written together since eighteen hundred and seventy-one.
SULLIVAN: Oh, that is patent balderdash!
GILBERT: Is it?
HELEN: Gentlemen, if we might keep things cordial, we may

make some progress. Arthur, can you really not see your way to setting this new piece?

SULLIVAN: Alas, Helen, I cannot.

HELEN: Cannot, or will not?

SULLIVAN: I am truly unable to set any piece that is so profoundly uncongenial to me.

HELEN: Uncongenial though it may be to you, I must remind you that we here are conducting a business.

SULLIVAN: And may I remind you, Helen, that I am not a machine.

HELEN: I would not suggest for one moment that you were.

SULLIVAN: You all seem to be treating me as a barrel-organ. You have but to turn my handle, and 'Hey Presto!' – out pops a tune!

(GILBERT, CARTE and HELEN *speak at once*.)

GILBERT: That's not strictly true.

CARTE: Arthur!

HELEN: Come now, that's unfair. (*She continues*.) You are both contractually obliged to supply a new work on request.

GILBERT: And the very act of signing a joint contract dictates that we must be businesslike.

HELEN: Yes, Mr Gilbert, and I was wondering whether you might not be able to solve our wee difficulty.

GILBERT: How, pray?

HELEN: By simply writing another libretto.

(SULLIVAN *looks worried*.)

GILBERT: That's out of the question. I have spent many long months working at this play, which I have every confidence will be the best we have yet produced at the Savoy, and to abandon it would be not only criminal, but wasteful.

HELEN: I see.

GILBERT: Now, had Sullivan lodged his complaint at an earlier date, that might have been a different matter.

SULLIVAN: I made my complaint the moment you presented me with the libretto.

GILBERT: The point being that I was unable to present you with the libretto until you returned from your Grand Tour of Europe.

SULLIVAN: That is neither here nor there.

GILBERT: No, Sullivan – indeed! I was here, and you were there! Ha!

HELEN: What I don't understand, Arthur, is why you cannot set this piece. You're our greatest composer – surely you can do anything.

SULLIVAN: How very kind you are, Helen; but I say again to you all, I am at the end of my tether. I have been repeating myself in this . . . class of work for too long, and I will not continue so to do.

GILBERT: Neither of us runs any risk of repeating himself, Sullivan. This is an entirely new story, quite unlike any other.

SULLIVAN: But, Gilbert, it bears a marked similarity to *The Sorcerer*. People are already saying we're repeating ourselves.

GILBERT: In what way is it similar to *The Sorcerer*?

SULLIVAN: Obviously, both involve characters who are transformed by the taking of a magic potion. A device which I continue to find utterly contrived.

GILBERT: Every theatrical performance is a contrivance, by its very nature.

SULLIVAN: Yes, but this piece consists entirely of an artificial and implausible situation.

GILBERT: If you wish to write a grand opera about a prostitute dying of consumption in a garret, I suggest you contact Mr Ibsen in Oslo. I am sure he will be able to furnish you with something suitably dull.

CARTE: Gilbert – please.

GILBERT: Hmm? I do beg your pardon, Miss Lenoir.

HELEN: Oh, no, granted.

SULLIVAN: The opportunity to treat a situation of tender, human and dramatic interest is one I long for more than anything else in the world.

GILBERT: If that is your sincere desire, I would be willing, with Carte's permission, to withdraw my services for one turn, to allow you to write a grand opera with a collaborator with whom you have a closer affinity than myself.

SULLIVAN: No, Gilbert.

GILBERT: I am in earnest, Sullivan.

CARTE: No doubt that is something we shall be pursuing in the future.
GILBERT: Indeed? Well, that is your prerogative, Carte.
HELEN: However, we are concerned with the present. Arthur, will you or will you not set Mr Gilbert's new and original work?
SULLIVAN: *Ma belle Hélène, ce n'est pas possible.*
HELEN: Truly?
SULLIVAN: I'm afraid so.
HELEN: That being the case . . . Mr Gilbert: would I be right in supposing that you remain unable to accommodate us?
GILBERT: Indeed, Miss Lenoir. I have had what I deem to be a good idea, and such ideas are not three a penny.
HELEN: What a pity. This will be a very sad day for many thousands of people.
(CARTE *takes out his pocket watch.*)
CARTE: Well, gentlemen . . . I don't know about you, but, speaking for myself, I could murder a pork chop.
(*He snaps his watch shut. Very long pause.*)
GILBERT: If you'll excuse me, I shall retrieve my hat.
(*He gets up, and goes through to* HELEN'*s office. She watches him. Then* CARTE *gets up, and stands by* HELEN'*s chair. Pause.* SULLIVAN *hesitates, then he too gets up and goes towards* HELEN'*s office.* GILBERT *is on his way back. They meet in the doorway.*)
SULLIVAN: Gilbert.
GILBERT: Sullivan.
(*He puts on his hat, and addresses* CARTE *and* HELEN.)
Good day to you both. No doubt we shall be in communication in the near future.
(CARTE *and* HELEN *speak at once.*)
CARTE: Gilbert.
HELEN: Good day, Mr Gilbert.
GILBERT: Good day.
(*He leaves the office.* SULLIVAN *returns from* HELEN'*s office. He is wearing his top hat. Pause.*)
SULLIVAN: You know where to find me.
HELEN: Arthur.
(*He leaves. Pause.* HELEN *sighs.*)

GILBERT's *study. Bright daylight.* GILBERT *is standing by his desk, smoking a cigar. Kitty comes in wearing her hat. During the following, they circle round the room.*

GILBERT: Where have you been?

KITTY: Shopping.

GILBERT (*sarcastic*): Surprising.

KITTY: I was in Knightsbridge . . . and guess what I saw!

GILBERT: An elephant gilding two lilies.

KITTY (*amused*): No.

GILBERT: I haven't the least idea.

KITTY: Three tiny Japanese ladies.

GILBERT: How do you know they were Japanese?

KITTY: Because they were wearing their funny dressing-gowns.

GILBERT: Had they just got up?

KITTY: No, there's a Japanese exhibition at Humphrey's Hall.

GILBERT: Oh, yes. Japanese village of some sort or other.

KITTY: Yes, yes, it sounds rather intriguing – might we visit?

GILBERT: No.

KITTY: But, Willie, the whole of London will be going.

GILBERT: Precisely.

(*He stubs out his cigar. They stand by the desk.*)

KITTY: Don't be so stubborn.

GILBERT: I have other things on my mind – you know that.

KITTY: Yes, I do know that, Willie, and I understand; but a little distraction will do you good.

(*She adjusts his lapel. He removes her hand.*)

GILBERT: Kitty: I don't want to be distracted.

KITTY: Yes, you do.

GILBERT: Oh, do I? You know my mind better than I do, do you?

KITTY: I know you better than you think I do, Willie.

GILBERT: Lucy, if you wish to visit Humphrey's Hall, by all means do so. But I shall not accompany you for all the tea in China.

(*He sits stubbornly at his desk. She looks at him for a moment, then walks briskly out of the room.*)

At the Japanese Exhibition. Members of London's middle classes wander about. In the distance a young woman sings a Japanese

song. A Japanese woman sits in a booth, working a spinning-wheel.
GILBERT *and* KITTY *stop to watch her for a few moments. Then they move on. A lady with a little girl takes their place.*

A CALLIGRAPHER *sits at another stall, writing on paper in classic Japanese style. The* GILBERTS *watch him.*
GILBERT: What are you writing, sir?
   (*The* CALLIGRAPHER *bows his head, and replies in Japanese.*)

GILBERT *and* KITTY *join a crowd at a stall laden with a variety of Japanese artefacts – fans, pots, vases, boxes, etc.*

Now the GILBERTS *are among a large audience watching a traditional Japanese dancer with her stylized movements and fan gestures. She is accompanied by the girl we have been hearing in the distance; she sings, and plays a stringed instrument, the shamisen. The spectators stand on all sides of the performers, who are on a small platform.* GILBERT *is clearly much taken with these ladies.*

A little later, in another part of the Exhibition. Two English ladies happen upon GILBERT *and* KITTY. *They turn out to be* GILBERT*'s maiden sisters,* MAUDE *and* FLORENCE.
MAUDE: Good afternoon, Lucy.
KITTY: Maude!
GILBERT: Good heavens! What are you two doing here?
MAUDE: How are you, Schwenck?
GILBERT: Hmm.
KITTY: How jolly! You must join us.
MAUDE: Unfortunately, we're just about to leave.
KITTY: Oh, what a pity.
GILBERT: What d'you make of it all?
MAUDE: It's quite entrancing.
FLORENCE: It's frightful!
   (GILBERT *and* KITTY *laugh.*)
KITTY: How's Mother?
MAUDE: Quite well.
FLORENCE: She's in bed.
KITTY: Oh.
FLORENCE: Come along, Maude. (*She leaves.*)

GILBERT: Oh, yes, Florence, we mustn't keep you. (*Raising his hat and bowing slightly.*) Good day to you.
KITTY: Do give her my best.
MAUDE (*going*): Of course. Well . . . *au revoir*.
KITTY: *Au revoir.*

Now a small group of people, mainly men, is watching two kendo fighters in full kit, slogging it out on a platform. GILBERT *and* KITTY *are among them.* GILBERT *is engaged by the fighting spirit.*

A traditional Japanese teahouse within the exhibition hall. Two ladies kneel on the raised platform, making the tea. Ladies and gentlemen, including GILBERT *and* KITTY, *sit at tables around the structure. The general public strolls by; wandering among them is an authentic Japanses water-bearer with a pole carrying two enormous vessels on his shoulders. A young lady in a white kimono arrives at the* GILBERTS' *table, and pours their green tea.*
KITTY: My goodness!
    (GILBERT *chortles.*)
    It's perfectly green.
GILBERT: Spinach water.
KITTY: Oh, Willie!
GILBERT (*to the* WAITRESS): Thank you very much.
WAITRESS (*bowing*): Sixerpen, prea.
GILBERT: I beg your pardon?
WAITRESS (*bowing*): Sixerpen, prea.
KITTY: Oh, she speaks English.
GILBERT: What did she say?
KITTY: She said, 'Sixpence, please.'
WAITRESS (*bowing*): Sixpence, please.
GILBERT: Ah, sixpence. (*He gives her sixpence.*) Thank you very much.
WAITRESS (*bowing*): *Arrigato, masaimas.* (*Bowing*) Sixpence, please.
    (GILBERT *beams.*)

A small theatre has been constructed. GILBERT *and* KITTY *are in the audience. It is a full house. Two kabuki actors are on the stage.*

Bright, bold-coloured costumes, wigs, make-up and back-cloth – a tree with a red sun. Gas footlights. The action is backed by a Japanese wind instrument and a drum.

The action: Two men. One, a lord, in a position of power. The other a lower person, a supplicant. The supplicant bows. He requests something. The lord sneers, provoking the supplicant to reach for his sword in anger. The lord leaps to his feet, shouting. The supplicant raises his shaking right hand in remorse. Wailing apology, he places his hands on the floor, and bows to the ground. The lord now harangues him, sarcastically and aggressively, until he finally provokes him. This time, the supplicant attacks the lord with his sword. Climax. Curtain.

   The audience is transfixed. KITTY *is horrified.* GILBERT *is fascinated. He joins in the applause.*

Later the same day. PIDGEON *enters* GILBERT*'s study, carrying a stepladder. He is wearing a green apron.*
PIDGEON: Here we are, sir.
   (*He crosses to* GILBERT, *who is holding a Japanese sword. He points it to a spot on the wall over the telephone booth.*)
GILBERT: There, Pidgeon.
PIDGEON: Very good, sir.
   (*He opens the ladders.* GILBERT *holds up the sword in mid-air.*)
GILBERT: *Comme ça.*
PIDGEON: Er – yes, sir.
   (*He climbs the ladder.* GILBERT *hands him the sword.*)
GILBERT: Show it to me.
   (PIDGEON *holds it against the wall.*)
   To your right.
   (PIDGEON *moves it.*)
   Bit more.
   (PIDGEON *moves it some more.*)
   Good – down a bit.
   (PIDGEON *moves it again.*)
   Down a bit.
   (PIDGEON *moves it yet again.*)
   There. Mark it there.

PIDGEON: Yes – sir. (*He takes a pencil from behind his ear, and marks it.*)
GILBERT: Give it to me.
PIDGEON (*doing so*): Thank you, sir. It's a fine-looking instrument, sir. Now would that be Spanish or Italian?
GILBERT: Neither, Pidgeon.
PIDGEON: Er, of course, sir.
 (PIDGEON *knocks a nail into the wall with a hammer.* GILBERT *watches.*)
GILBERT: Good.
 (*He hands* PIDGEON *the sword.* PIDGEON *hangs it up. He looks to* GILBERT *for approval.*)
 Excellent. Thank you. (GILBERT *walks away.*)
PIDGEON: Thank you, sir. (*He proceeds down the ladder.*)

GILBERT'S MOTHER's *house. His sister* MAUDE *is tending her indoor plants. The camera pans round the gloomy, musty, cluttered room, past the mantelpiece laden with bric-à-brac.* FLORENCE *is playing an upright piano – improvising a doleful dirge. The camera continues past her on to a heavily draped window and then yet more layers of clutter. It finally comes to rest on Gilbert's* MOTHER, *a handsome if withered old lady in a bonnet and shawl. She is propped up on numerous pillows in a huge bed. An invalid table sits on the bed, over her legs. On it, caught in a narrow shaft of afternoon light, is a wooden Japanese vessel.*

 FLORENCE *concludes her impromptu cacophony.* MAUDE *is now attending to some dried flowers. Pause.*

MOTHER: Do we suppose that Lucy is with child? (*She raises an ear-trumpet to her ear.*)
MAUDE: I beg your pardon, Mama?
MOTHER: Lucy. Is she *enceinte* . . . with child?
MAUDE: Why ever would you think that?
FLORENCE: One wouldn't have said she was sickly. Although she did ask after you, Mama.
 (*She starts playing a chirpy tune on the piano.* GILBERT'S MOTHER *watches her suspiciously. The tune grinds to a halt.*)
MOTHER: What did he say?
MAUDE: Who?
MOTHER: Schwenck.

(FLORENCE *gets up suddenly.*)
FLORENCE (*neurotically*): He said nothing, Mama. Nothing. Nothing. Absolutely nothing.
(*She storms out of the room, slamming the door. Pause.*)
MAUDE (*coming to the bed*): Your dear son said very little, and what he did say I have already told you. Now, do you care for this, or not?
(*She picks up the Japanese artefact.*)
MOTHER: It is merely a piece of wood.
MAUDE: Very well, I shall keep it for my collection. (*She goes to the door and opens it.*)
MOTHER: Maude!
MAUDE (*stopping*): Yes, Mama?
MOTHER: Never bear a humorous baby.
MAUDE: I shall endeavour not to, Mama. (*She leaves the room, closing the door behind her.*)

Late at night, GILBERT, *wearing his nightcap and dressing-gown, is pacing restlessly round his study. He has a glass of whisky in his hand.* (*Music cue 8 begins and ends.*) *Suddenly, the Japanese sword falls off the wall, and lands on the floor with a clatter. He picks it up and looks at it; then he plays with it. First he does a bit of swashbuckling. Then follows a Japanese improvisation, echoing the kendo and kabuki performances at the exhibition.*

GILBERT *puts the sword down on his desk.* (*Music cue 9 begins.*) *He looks at it. He stops. Pause.* (*Music ends.*) *He thinks . . . A gleam appears in his eye. He has a flash of inspiration. In the distance, we hear a fanfare, followed by a tune. A smile breaks out on* GILBERT'*s face. We are listening to the opening bars of Ko-Ko's entrance in Act 1 of* The Mikado. *We cut to the stage – the setting for Act 1: the courtyard of Ko-Ko's official residence. At first we see the chorus of noblemen in silhouette; then the lights come up swiftly as they dance round the stage in symmetrical formation.*
CHORUS (*sings*):
> Behold the Lord High Executioner!
> A personage of noble rank and title –
> A dignified and potent officer,
> Whose functions are particularly vital!

> (*They illustrate this with a chopping gesture.*)
> Defer, defer,
> To the Lord High Executioner!
> Defer, defer,
> To the noble Lord, to the noble Lord,
> To the Lord High Executioner!
> (*Upstage, two red sliding doors open quickly to reveal* GROSSMITH *and a small boy.* GROSSMITH *is playing Ko-Ko. He carries a huge Japanese sword on his right shoulder. He proceeds downstage, followed by the boy, who sits on the floor.*)

GROSSMITH (*sings*):
> Taken from the county jail
> By a set of curious chances;
> Liberated then on bail,
> On my own recognizances;
> Wafted by a fav'ring gale
> As one sometimes is in trances,
> To a height that few can scale,
> Save by long and weary dances;
> Surely, never had a male
> Under such-like circumstances
> So adventurous a tale,
> Which may rank with most romances.
> (*The following sung ensemble.*)
> Taken from the county jail
> By a set of curious chances;
> Surely, never had a male
> So adventurous a tale.

CHORUS (*sings*):
> Taken from the county jail,
> Liberated then on bail
> Surely, never had a male
> So adventurous a tale.

SULLIVAN'*s study. Day.* GILBERT *is sitting on the sofa. He is reading to* SULLIVAN, *who moves around behind him with animated enthusiasm, laughing frequently. He is smoking a cigarette.*

GILBERT (*reads*): The Mikado or The Town of Titipu.

(SULLIVAN *laughs.*)

Act One. Scene: Courtyard of Ko-Ko's palace in Titipu. Japanese nobles discovered standing and sitting in attitudes suggested by native drawings. Chorus:
 If you want to know who we are,
 We are gentlemen of Japan.
 On many a vase and jar –
 On many a screen and fan,
 We figure in lively paint:
 Our attitudes queer and quaint –
 You're wrong if you think it ain't.
 (SULLIVAN *guffaws*.)
 If you think we are worked by strings,
 Like a Japanese marionette,
 You don't understand these things:
 It is simply Court etiquette.
 Perhaps you suppose this throng
 Can't keep it up all day long?
 If that's your idea, you're wrong.
Enter Nanki-Poo, in great excitement. He carries a native guitar on his back and a bundle of ballads in his hand.
 (SULLIVAN *laughs, and sits on a chair.*)

Recitative, Nanki-Poo:
Gentlemen, I pray you tell me
Where a lovely maiden dwelleth,
Named Yum-Yum, the ward of Ko-Ko?
In pity speak – oh, speak, I pray you!

Day. In his study, GILBERT *and* KITTY *sit on either side of the fireplace. A fire blazes.* GILBERT *has his feet on a stool. He is reading to* KITTY, *who listens reflectively. (Music cue 10 starts.)*
GILBERT (*reads*): I hurried back at once, in the hope of finding Yum-Yum at liberty to listen to my protestations.

Pish-Tush: It is true that Ko-Ko was condemned to death for flirting, but he was reprieved at the last moment, and raised to the exalted rank of Lord High Executioner, under the following remarkable circumstances.

Song, Pish-Tush:

Our great Mikado, virtuous man,
When he to rule our land began,
Resolved to try
A plan whereby
Young men might best be steadied.
So he decreed in words succinct,

That all who flirted, leered or winked
(Unless connubially linked)
Should forthwith be beheaded.

And I expect you'll all agree
That he was right to so decree.
And I am right,
And you are right,
And all is right as right can be!

This stern decree, you'll understand,
Caused great dismay throughout the land!
For young and old
And shy and bold
Were equally affected.
The youth who winked a roving eye,
Or breathed a non-connubial sigh,
Was thereupon condemned to die –
He usually objected.

And you'll allow, as I expect,
That he was right to so object.
And I am right,
And you are right,
And everything is quite correct.

And so we straight let out on bail
A convict from the county jail,
Whose head was next
On some pretext
Condemnëd to be mown off,
And made him Headsman, for we said,
'Who's next to be decapited
Cannot cut off another's head
Until he's cut his own off.'

And we are right, I think you'll say,
To argue in this kind of way;
And I am right,
And you are right,
And all is right – too-looral-lay!

Chorus. End of song.
KITTY: Highly amusing, Willie.
GILBERT: Fatuous.
KITTY: Oh. Surely Arthur likes it?
(*Music cue 10 ends.*)
GILBERT: He hasn't said otherwise.
KITTY (*subtly; dry irony*): It certainly is rich in human emotion and probability.
(GILBERT *is apparently oblivious to her irony.*)
GILBERT: Hardly.
(KITTY *sighs. The merest hint of pique.* GILBERT *reads.*)
Enter Pooh-Bah.

Music cue 11 starts. An elderly, bearded Waiter makes his way through a bustling restaurant, bearing three pint glasses of stout on a tray. All the diners are men.

A caption:
   'February 12th 1885. News reaches London of the killing of General Gordon by the Mahdi's troops at Khartoum.'
The Waiter passes behind a partition. GROSSMITH, LELY *and* RUTLAND BARRINGTON, *another Savoy actor, are having lunch.* GROSSMITH *and* BARRINGTON *are eating oysters. All are smartly dressed in suits.* GROSSMITH *is wearing his pince-nez. The Waiter serves the stouts.*
LELY: It's a tragedy.
GROSSMITH: It is.
LELY: *Que bruto.*
BARRINGTON: Absolutely. He simply hasn't played with a straight bat.
LELY: Who's that?
GROSSMITH: His Majesty, the Mahdi.
LELY: Ah, yes.
GROSSMITH: No, it just isn't cricket.
BARRINGTON: Quite so. It's completely contrary to the rules of engagement. The man was surrounded on all sides, and massacred mercilessly.
GROSSMITH: 'What full fortune doth the thick-lips owe.'
BARRINGTON: What does that mean?

GROSSMITH: Philistine. It baffles me that you're baffled, Barrington.
BARRINGTON: Mm?
GROSSMITH: The Hottentot in the desert doesn't play cricket. His natural habitation being the jungly-bungly tree, he is as yet hardly able to walk upright, don't you know.
BARRINGTON (*chortling*): We strive to bring them civilization, and this is their gratitude.
LELY: Did you know that fifty-six families were slaughtered on the Island of Skye?
GROSSMITH: Really?
LELY: Mm.
GROSSMITH: When was that?
LELY: In eighty-two, I think.
GROSSMITH: And who perpetrated the outrage, pray?
LELY: Ah, merely the, er – English militia.
GROSSMITH: Extraordinary.
LELY: *Bon appetito.*
   (BARRINGTON *downs his last oyster.*)
BARRINGTON: Shall we indulge in another dozen?
GROSSMITH: I rather think we ought, don't you?

BARRINGTON: I think we might. Would you care for a second fish, Lely?
(LELY *laughs*.)
GROSSMITH: Or a veritable shoal, perhaps?
LELY (*to* GROSSMITH): I've had an ample sufficiency, thank you very much, ma wee man.
(*Pause*.)
BARRINGTON: I have an appointment with Carte this afternoon.
GROSSMITH: At what hour?
BARRINGTON: Five o'clock.
GROSSMITH: Curious. I shall be with him at half-past four.
LELY: That's funny, I don't have a meeting with him at four o'clock.
BARRINGTON: And it is my firm intention to prise open his purse.
GROSSMITH: It will take a far stronger man than you, Mr Barrington, to fulfil that Herculean labour.
(BARRINGTON *chortles*.)
BARRINGTON: And what's your mission, Captain Grossmith?
GROSSMITH: Oh, there are certain matters. (*He tackles another oyster. Music cue 11 ends*.)

CARTE'S *office*. CARTE *and* GROSSMITH *face each other across the desk*.
CARTE: I should rather like to offer you an increase in salary, George.
GROSSMITH: Oh? Indeed?
CARTE: Indeed.
GROSSMITH: That's most benevolent of you, Mr Carte.
CARTE: It's no less than you deserve, George.
GROSSMITH: Thank you. And by how much, might one enquire?
CARTE: By seven-and-a-half per cent.
GROSSMITH: Mm. Seven-and-a-half. Now that would work out at, er . . .
CARTE: Thirty pounds per week.
GROSSMITH: Thirty? Mm, I see. Well, thirty pounds per week wasn't quite the sum I had in mind as I wended my weary way here this afternoon.

CARTE: Indeed?
GROSSMITH: As that would be three consecutive productions with only a negligible increase.
CARTE: I don't consider an increase of two pounds per week over twelve months negligible, George.
GROSSMITH: One might have thought that the name of George Grossmith, my not inconsiderable contribution, would have been more favourably recognized.
CARTE: You do receive considerably more than anybody else, George.
GROSSMITH: Do I?
CARTE: Mm.
(*Pause.*)
We should be terribly sorry to lose you.
(*A gesture of mock-sympathy from* GROSSMITH.)
Gilbert has written you a particularly fine part in the new piece.
GROSSMITH: Precisely – as one would expect. However, I should judge an increase of a paltry two pounds per week to be wholly unacceptable, not to mention mildly insulting, if one may say so.
CARTE (*peeved*): And what figure had you in mind, Mr Grossmith?
(*Pause.*)
GROSSMITH: Er . . . Forgive me, I seem to have lost my train of thought.
(*Music cue 12 starts.* GROSSMITH *touches his forehead and leans forward. He breathes heavily. He takes off his pince-nez. Then he sighs deeply.* CARTE *leans forward.*)
CARTE: Are you unwell, George?
GROSSMITH: I fear I may have come over a bit queer. Most embarrassing.
CARTE (*getting up*): You must take a little brandy.
GROSSMITH (*heavy breathing*): Oh!!

A little later. Still in CARTE's *office.* CARTE *is standing over* BARRINGTON, *who looks uncomfortable.* HELEN *comes in from her office, carrying a decanter of water and a glass.*
HELEN: A little water clears us of this deed. (*She pours some out.*)

BARRINGTON: I blame Grossmith for this.
HELEN: Only Grossmith? (*She gives him the glass.*)
BARRINGTON: Thank you, Helen. Confounded glutton.
(*He takes a sip.* CARTE *sit at his desk.*)
CARTE: Are you feeling better?
BARRINGTON: Oh, I do beg your pardon – this is awfully embarrassing.
CARTE: Not at all, Rutty. Now, why don't we return to the subject of your salary?
BARRINGTON: Oh . . . yes . . . Well, I must declare that I'm . . . rather at a loss for words, D'Oyly.
HELEN: Excuse me. (*She starts to leave, but stops . . .*)
BARRINGTON (*ill*): Ooooh. Oh, I do beg your pardon. This is a bally nightmare, dammit. (*He rushes out of the room.*) I shall be in my dressing-room.
(*He slams the door behind him. Music cue 12 ends.*)
HELEN: The more I see of men, the more I admire dogs. (*She goes to her office.*)

Later still. Now it is LEONORA*'s turn to see* CARTE. *They sit on either side of his desk.*
CARTE: I'm soon to have a meeting concerning the cast for the next opera.
LEONORA: Yes, indeed. And I've heard a little rumour that perhaps I shall be playing the part of a fourteen-year-old schoolgirl.
CARTE: Someone has been telling tales.
LEONORA (*giggling*): They have indeed, Mr Carte.
CARTE: Mr Gilbert will be very angry.
(LEONORA *giggles again.*)
With reference to your engagement for the opera . . . I have a great concern about your little weakness.
(*Pause.*)
LEONORA: I'm a little shocked, Mr Carte. I really do believe that my behaviour this last year has been exemplary.
CARTE: I'm pleased to say your tendency has improved, but I am concerned about the future.
(*A few streets away, a barrel-organ starts to play.*)

LEONORA: Yes . . . you're perhaps suggesting, Mr Carte, that I shan't be performing in the next production . . .
CARTE: Yes, I'm afraid I am. But the outcome of that, Leonora, is in your own hands.
(*Pause.*)
LEONORA: Sometimes, Mr Carte, I can be a very silly young woman.
CARTE: You have an extraordinary talent. It saddens me beyond measure to see someone throw it away.
LEONORA: I assure you, Mr Carte, that I shall be in tip-top form. (*She smiles.*)
CARTE: I'm very pleased to hear that. Much relieved. (*Pause.*) Do we have an understanding?
LEONORA: Yes, we do, Mr Carte.
(*Pause. She looks at him.*)
CARTE (*softly*): Good.
(*Pause.* LEONORA *looks down.*)

LELY *sits in his dressing-room, at his place. He is wearing his red soldier's tunic.* BUTT *is dressing a wig.* LELY *mixes something in a glass.*

LELY (*sings*):
> Charlie, Charlie,
> Wha' wouldn'a follow thee?
> King o' the Highland hearts,
> Bonnie Prince Charlie!
> (*He raises his glass to Bonnie Prince Charlie, and gargles.*
> TEMPLE *is heard along the corridor.*)

TEMPLE: Chop-chop, Butt. How long do we have?
(*He arrives, giving his cane to* BUTT.)
BUTT: Eight minutes, Mr Temple.
TEMPLE: Oh, jolly good. Shocking news from Khartoum!
(LELY *spits his gargle into a chamber pot.*)
LELY: Indeed.
TEMPLE: Unbearable. Something will have to be done, *tout suite*.
LELY: Absolutely.
(TEMPLE *turns round so that* BUTT *can remove his overcoat.*)
TEMPLE: Mrs Temple hit the nail on the head this afternoon, as per usual.
LELY: Oh? What did she say?
TEMPLE: 'The nation loses a hero, but the family loses a loved one.'
LELY: Oh, how apt.
(BUTT *removes* TEMPLE*'s jacket.*)
TEMPLE: A perspicacious woman is Mrs Temple. (*He taps his hat*). Hat!
(BUTT *removes it.*)
Consider this, my dear Butt. Is it not the inevitable fate of the professional soldier that he may perish on the field of battle?
(BUTT *is undoing* TEMPLE*'s necktie.*)
BUTT: Indeed, sir.
LELY: But, Dickie, have you heard the real news of the day?
(BUTT *is unbuttoning* TEMPLE*'s waistcoat.*)
TEMPLE: Yes, the Fenian bomb – oh, dreadful!
LELY: No. Grossmith and Barrington.
TEMPLE: What?
LELY: They're off tonight.
TEMPLE: No!
LELY: Yes.

TEMPLE: Both of them?
LELY: Yes.
TEMPLE: Why?
LELY: Oysters.
TEMPLE (*gasping*): Oh!
LELY: Mm, we shared luncheon together.
TEMPLE: Did you swallow?
LELY: No, I chose the sole.
TEMPLE: Off the bone?
LELY: Yes, it was rather succulent.
TEMPLE: Wise man. Oysters can kill, you know. (*He pulls down his braces.*)
LELY: Oh, unquestionably.
TEMPLE: I had an aunt, choked on a scallop at Herne Bay.
(*Does* BUTT *snigger?* TEMPLE *looks at him.*)
LELY: Really?
TEMPLE: Tragic.
LELY: Oh, dear. Yes, they were away to see Carte.
TEMPLE: Oh, really? (*He sits in his place.*)
LELY: Mm.
TEMPLE: Will you be lobbying?
LELY: No, I'll just wait for my summons.
TEMPLE: Quite right, dear boy. One should be rewarded on one's merits, not on one's ability to ingratiate oneself with the management. Particularly when the management have difficulty in locating the relative whereabouts of the arse and the elbow.
(LELY *chuckles.*)
Serves them both right.
(TEMPLE *gets up and closes the door. We are outside.* SHRIMP *arrives immediately, and knocks.*)
TEMPLE (*within*): Enter!
(SHRIMP *opens the door.* TEMPLE *has dropped his trousers to reveal suspenders.* LELY *is gargling, and spits into the potty.*)
SHRIMP: Five minutes, please, Mr Temple, Mr Lely.
LELY: Thank you, Shrimp.
TEMPLE: *Merci, Crevette!!*
(SHRIMP *closes the door, and leaves.*)

SULLIVAN's *study. Day. A rehearsal.* GROSSMITH, BARRINGTON *and another actor,* BOVILL, *stand around* SULLIVAN *at his piano.* GROSSMITH *is smoking a cigarette.*

GROSSMITH (*sings*):
>And so,
>Although
>I'm ready to go,
>Yet recollect
>'Twere disrespect

SULLIVAN: *Dolce.*

GROSSMITH (*sings*):
>Did I neglect
>To thus effect

SULLIVAN: Expansive!

GROSSMITH (*sings*):
>This aim direct,
>So I object.

SULLIVAN: Good.

BARRINGTON (*sings*):
>And so,
>Although

SULLIVAN (*simultaneously*): Rutty, temper your volume, please.

BARRINGTON (*quieter*):
  I wish to go
  And gently pine
  To brightly shine
SULLIVAN (*simultaneously*): And now! Good!
BARRINGTON: And take the line
  Of a hero fine
  With grief condign
  I must decline.
  (*During* BOVILL*'s following verse,* GROSSMITH *does a comic dance.*)
BOVILL (*sings*):
  And go
  And show
  Both friend and foe
  How much you dare.
  I'm quite aware
  It's your affair,
  Yet I declare
  I'd take your share
  But I don't –
  (SULLIVAN *stops abruptly.*)
SULLIVAN: Bovill, that's very good, but, er . . . I've gone to considerable pains to provide you with triplets.
BOVILL: Triplets, Sir Arthur, yes.
BARRINGTON: And on his salary. (*Laughing.*)
SULLIVAN (*amused*): Rutty, please!
BARRINGTON: Apology.
SULLIVAN (*still amused*): Consequently, if you would be so kind as to trip.
BOVILL: Of course, Sir Arthur.
SULLIVAN: Thank you. One, two, three, four.
  (*An amused glance at* BARRINGTON, *who laughs.*)
BOVILL (*sings*):
  And go
  And show
  Both friend and foe
  How much you dare.
  I'm quite aware

>   It's your affair
>   Yet I declare
>   I'd take your share,
>   But I don't much care.
>   (SULLIVAN *stops playing*.)

SULLIVAN: Now you see, Bovill: very much better.
BOVILL: Thank you, Sir Arthur.
GROSSMITH: The new man's doing awfully well.
BARRINGTON: Quite splendid.
BOVILL: Thank you, gentlemen.
BARRINGTON: Breathe, Bovill, breathe.
BOVILL: Yes.
SULLIVAN: Yes, and *piano*, Barrington – *piano*.
BARRINGTON: I'll do my best.
GROSSMITH: As many p's as you can muster, Rutland.
>   (BARRINGTON *chortles*.)

SULLIVAN: Without landing us all in the soup. One, two, three, *four*!
>   (*During the following he turns and grins at* BARRINGTON.)

BOVILL (*sings*):
>   And go
>   And show
>   Both friends and foe
>   How much you dare.
>   I'm quite aware
>   It's your affair
>   Yet I declare
>   I'd take your share
>   But I don't much care.

SULLIVAN: And going on –!
>   (*The following sung ensemble*.)

BARRINGTON (*sings*):
>   I must decline,
>   I must decline,
>   I must decline,
>   I must decline,
>   I must decline,
>   I must decline –

BOVILL (*sings*):
> I'd take your share,
> But I don't much care,
> I'd take your share,
> But I don't much care,
> I'd take your share,
> But I don't much care,
> Much care, I don't
> Much care, I don't much care –

GROSSMITH (*sings*):
> So I object
> So I object,
> So I object,
> So I object,
> So I object,
> So I object –

ALL THREE (*sing*):
> To sit in solemn silence in a –
> (SULLIVAN *stops playing, and claps his hands.*)

SULLIVAN: Gentlemen: *un poco piu vivo* – mm? Now, before the double bar line, it's (*beating time*) one, two, three, four; and afterwards it's (*beating time*) one-two-three-four. Clear? Very well. From here, please. One-two-three-four! –
(*Following three parts sung at once.*)

BOVILL (*sings*):
> Care, I don't much care,
> I don't much care –

BARRINGTON (*sings*):
> . . . I must decline,
> I must decline –

GROSSMITH (*sings*):
> So I object,
> So I object –

ALL THREE (*sing*):
> To sit in solemn silence in a dull, dark dock –

SULLIVAN: Good!

ALL THREE (*sing*):
> In a pestilential prison, with a life-long lock,
> Awaiting the sensation of a short, sharp shock –

SULLIVAN: Consonants!
ALL THREE (*sing*):
   From a cheap and chippy chopper on a big black block!
   To sit in solemn silence in a dull, dark dock –
SULLIVAN: More! Good.
ALL THREE (*sing*):
   In a pestilential prison with a life-long lock,
   Awaiting the sensation of a short, sharp shock,
   From a cheap and chippy chopper on a big black block!
   A dull, dark dock,
   A life-long lock,
   A short, sharp shock,
   A big black block!
   To sit in solemn silence
   In a pestilential prison
   And awaiting the sensation
   From a cheap and chippy chopper
   On a big –
   Black –
   Block!!
   (*As they reach the climax, they erupt into enthusiastic laughter.*
   LOUIS *has entered with a tray of coffee.*)
GROSSMITH: Bravo.
BOVILL: Goodness.
BARRINGTON: Splendid!
SULLIVAN (*getting up*): Excellent! Louis, *wir haben etwas Kaffee.*
LOUIS: Your coffee is ready, Sir Arthur.
SULLIVAN: Thank you.
   (*They all move towards the coffee.*)
BOVILL: My word . . .
SULLIVAN (*to* GROSSMITH): Gee-Gee . . .
GROSSMITH: First rate. (*He sits on the sofa.*)
SULLIVAN: Er, Rutty, do go through.
BARRINGTON: Thanks, old chap.
   (*He puts a cigar in his mouth, and joins* GROSSMITH.)

Music cue 13 starts. A small fitting-room at the Savoy. Day.
MADAME LEON, *the ladies' costumier, is fitting a white Japanese under-garment on* SIBYL GREY, *a young actress.* SIBYL *is standing*

on a small box. JESSIE *and* LEONORA *are present.* MADAME LEON *is an attractive middle-aged Londoner. She has two assistants: a diminutive middle-aged lady (*MISS MORTON*), and a young girl (*ALICE*). Everybody except* SIBYL *is wearing a hat.*

Whilst MADAME LEON *adjusts the garment,* SIBYL *holds up her hands, which are hidden inside her sleeves.*
SIBYL: Do one's hands remain within, Madame Leon?
MME LEON: Oh, no, my dear. No, no, no, no, no. Look . . . here.
 (*She pulls down* SIBYL*'s sleeve to reveal her hand.*)
 Comme ça.
SIBYL: Oh, I see.
MME LEON: *Voilà.*
 (SIBYL *giggles.* JESSIE *sits down with a cup of tea.*)
 Are you still troubled by your understandings, Miss Bond?
JESSIE: I'm in much pain this afternoon.
MME LEON: I'm so sorry to hear it. (*She returns her attention to the costume.*) Oh, *très jolie, très jolie – superbe, bon.*
SIBYL: Such exquisite embroidery.
 (LEONORA *feels* SIBYL*'s garment.*)
LEONORA: What are you wearing underneath your gown, Sibyl?

SIBYL: Only my frillies.
LEONORA: Mmm!
MME LEON: Alas: no corsets, I'm afraid to say. (*To her young assistant:*) Alice – *vite*!
LEONORA: Oh, shall we be revealing a little, Madame Leon?
MME LEON: I certainly hope not, Miss Braham!
LEONORA: Oh, what a pity.
(*She gives* SIBYL *a naughty look.* SIBYL *giggles.*)
MME LEON: Oh, do take care, Miss Morton!
(*Her assistants are preparing to move a kimono.*)
SIBYL: It makes one rather drowsy.
LEONORA: Mm, it does look comfortable, Sibyl.
SIBYL: Indeed it is.
MME LEON: *La kimono! Doucement, doucement.* Gently, gently.
(MISS MORTON *and* ALICE *fit the kimono on Sibyl.*)
LEONORA: Oh! The silk is sublime, Madame Leon.
(JESSIE *gets up, and watches more closely.*)
MME LEON: Indeed. From Mr Liberty's store, don't you know? Bona fide Japanese, and just a *soupçon* from Gay Paris.
(LEONORA *puts the silk to her cheek.*)
LEONORA: *C'est magnifique.*
MME LEON: *Ah, oui!* (*She chuckles.*)
(MISS MORTON *ties* SIBYL*'s waist cord.*)
JESSIE: Is one to presume one is to be prevented from wearing one's corset, Madame Leon?
MME LEON: Miss Bond, none of the ladies shall be wearing corsets during the performance.
JESSIE: That's simply preposterous!
MME LEON: Our aim is to emulate the Japanese ladies, and Japanese ladies are as thin as thread paper, inasmuch a Roman column as opposed to a Grecian urn.
JESSIE: Quite so.
(MADAME LEON *takes over* SIBYL*'s waist cord.*)
I fear for my reputation, don't you know.
MME LEON: Miss Bond, I am following Mr Gilbert's instructions. Mr Gilbert desires the Japanese appearance, and that which Mr Gilbert desires, Mr Gilbert must have. *Fait accompli.*
JESSIE: One can hardly cut a dash in this . . . dressing-gown.

LEONORA: Oh, do stop fussing, Jessie – please. It's delightful, Madame Leon.

MME LEON: Thank you, Miss Braham.

JESSIE: It's shapeless.

MME LEON: Yes, Miss Bond, it is shapeless. Japanese ladies are most shapeless. But there is no reason for you ladies to be shapeless. I have devised a solution – if I may crave your indulgence.

(MISS MORTON *is holding another garment.*)

Miss Morton . . . Er, er, Miss Grey, would you kindly raise your arms?

SIBYL: Of course.

(*She does so. They fit her with a kind of corset which looks like a ready-tied Japanese sash, or 'obi'.*)

MME LEON: *Merci, merci.* Now, the bow goes at the back, the sash at the front, lined with calico. (*To* SIBYL:) Now, *tournez. Tournez, s'il vous plaît.*

(SIBYL *turns, giggling.* MISS MORTON *laces up the contraption.*)

Now this may be laced as tightly as you require. *Tournez . . . à gauche, à gauche.*

(SIBYL *turns back.*)

Oui. So you see, in effect, it is a corset.

(JESSIE *inspects it.*)

JESSIE: Where's the whalebone?

MME LEON: There are no bones, Miss Bond.

JESSIE: Well, Madame Leon, I do fear that if there are no bones, then it is plainly not a corset.

MME LEON: No, Miss Bond, it is not a corset; but it may serve for a corset. It may give you the shape you desire. Tighter, please, Miss Morton – tighter.

(MISS MORTON *tightens it.*)

JESSIE: I cannot appear on stage without a corset.

SIBYL: It certainly feels like a corset, Jessie.

LEONORA: You do resemble a birthday gift, Sibyl. I could eat you.

(SIBYL *giggles.*)

MME LEON: Do forgive me, Miss Bond. One is working to the best of one's abilities . . . although I fear sometimes it is not always appreciated.

(*She adjusts the kimono. There is an embarrassed silence. Music cue 13 ends.*)

The same fitting-room. Another day. WILHELM, *the gentlemen's costume designer, is removing a Japanese top-garment from* LELY, *who is standing on the little box.* GILBERT *is sitting watching. So is* GROSSMITH, *who is wearing his pince-nez, his Japanese costume and his own top hat.* GILBERT*'s hat is beside him on a table.*

GILBERT: And that is the 'hori'. Am I correct, Wilhelm?
WILHELM: Quite so, Mr Gilbert.
GILBERT: As opposed to the 'zori', which is the stocking, is it not?
WILHELM: No, the stockings are the 'tarbi', sir.
(*He adjusts* LELY*'s remaining garment.*)
GILBERT: Ah, 'tarbi'. The sandals are the 'zori'.
WILHELM: Exactly so.
GILBERT: I'm beginning to get the measure of this, Grossmith.
GROSSMITH: Hmm.
LELY: Mr Gilbert.
GILBERT: Lely?
LELY: Is this to be the length of my gown for Nanki-Poo?
(*The gown stops at his thighs. He is wearing long black stockings.*)
GILBERT: I believe so. Wilhelm?
WILHELM: Indeed it is.
GILBERT (*to* LELY): Yes.
LELY: Do you not consider it to be perhaps a little too short?
GILBERT: Too short for what?
LELY: For propriety. Might it not be rather unseemly?
GILBERT: I'm sorry – unseemly to whom?
LELY: To the audience of the Savoy Theatre, sir.
GILBERT: Hmm. I shouldn't have thought so. In any case, I shall be the judge of that.
WILHELM: And rest assured, Mr Lely, my designs are properly researched, and authentic to the last thread.
LELY: Hm. Well, no offence to you, Mr Wilhelm, but your properly authentic costume seems to have left me rather in the buff somewhat.
GROSSMITH: Quite.

WILHELM: No more in the buff than Japanese peasants have been for the last eight hundred years, Mr Lely.

LELY: May I draw your attention to the fact, Mr Wilhelm, that I am not actually a Japanese peasant?

GILBERT: No, you're a Scotch actor who's taking the part of a Japanese prince who is posing as an itinerant minstrel.

GROSSMITH: Lely, I would be only too happy for the tailor here to chop off some of my surplus, and stitch it to the hem of your kilt.

(LELY *snorts a laugh*.)

GILBERT: Thank you, Grossmith. I am sure we shall reap the benefits of your remonstrations in the fullness of time.

GROSSMITH: Hm.

LELY: Yes, Gee-Gee. Do you not agree with me that this garment is rather vulgar?

GROSSMITH: I do, as it happens.

WILHELM: Mr Grossmith, kindly oblige me by removing your hat!

GROSSMITH: Why, sir – are you ready for me?

WILHELM: Would that I were, sir. And I'll thank you not to refer to my designs as vulgar, Mr Lely.

LELY: Mr Wilhelm, to my eyes, your designs are not only vulgar, but obscene.

WILHELM: How dare you, sir!

GILBERT: Strong words, Lely. What the deuce d'you mean?

LELY: Mr Gilbert, I'm a respectably married man and I love my wife dearly. Now, one of the few pleasures that she has enjoyed since the untimely demise of my beloved mother-in-law has been to watch me perform upon the stage; but I am not prepared to allow her to suffer the embarrassment of seeing me flaunted before the public like a half-dressed performing dog!

GILBERT: You have my sympathies, Lely. But unfortunately your avocation as an actor compels you on occasion to endure the most ignominious indignities, as Grossmith will doubtless testify.

GROSSMITH: Without question, sir.

WILHELM: Mr Lely, let me be clear. I will not alter one stitch of your costume to protect the sensibilities of your wife, your children, or any other member of your unfortunate family.

(LELY *leans into* WILHELM's *face.*)

LELY: Mr Wilhelm, I would strongly advise you not to speak of my family in such a despicable manner.

WILHELM: Sir, will you remove your corset?

LELY: I beg your pardon?!

WILHELM: Kindly remove your corset, Mr Lely – it'll spoil the hang of the cloth. (WILHELM *moves to a table, where he flicks through his* Mikado *sketchbook.*)

LELY: Mr Gilbert . . . I never perform without my corset.

GILBERT: What, never?

LELY (*a half-laugh*): I'm afraid not, sir.

GILBERT: Why not?

LELY: One cannot produce the required vocal vigour without the necessary diaphragmatical support that the corset affords.

GILBERT: Come, come, Lely. This is not grand opera in Milan. It is merely low burlesque in a small theatre on the banks of the River Thames. You have a fine, strong voice which will be more than adequate for our purposes, with or without the corset. Kindly remove it this instant.

WILHELM: You may retire behind the screen if you wish.

LELY: Very well, sir. (*He proceeds to the screen, but stops by it.*) But may I just say that in five years of loyal service to this company, I have never, until this moment, lodged a single complaint. (*He swans behind the screen.*)

GILBERT (*winking at* GROSSMITH): Your noble restraint has been much appreciated.

(LELY *leans out for a moment from behind the screen. He is more undressed.*)

LELY: Thank you, sir.

The Savoy Theatre. The Mikado *in performance – another 'flash-forward', like Ko-Ko's entrance earlier. The strings play the pizzicato introduction, and* LELY *sings Nanki-Poo's song. The Chorus of Noblemen is grouped round him, some standing, others kneeling. They flutter their fans.* LELY *carries a pretend shamisen, which he 'strums' stagily.*

LELY (*sings*):

A wand'ring minstrel, I –

A thing of shreds and patches,
Of ballads, songs and snatches,
And dreamy lullaby!
My catalogue is long,
Through ev'ry passion ranging,
And to your humours changing
I tune my supple song!
I tune my supple song!
(*The* CHORUS *close their fans in unison.*)
Are you in sentimental mood?
I'll sigh with you.
(*The gentlemen of the* CHORUS *all sigh in unison.*)
Oh, – sorrow!
On maiden's coldness do you brood?
I'll do so, too –
Oh, sorrow, sorrow!
I'll charm your willing ears
With songs of lovers' fears,
While sympathetic tears
My cheeks bedew
(*The noblemen of the* CHORUS *all point to their eyes.*)
Oh, sorrow, sorrow!

The Savoy Theatre. A rehearsal. The set for The Sorcerer *is standing. A temporary platform extends from the stage into the auditorium, which is empty. Large, primitive electric lamps. Watched by a lady chorister,* JOHN D'AUBAN, *the choreographer, wearing ballet tights and smoking his pipe, cavorts and pirouettes about the stage.* SEYMOUR, *the stage manager, puts out chairs.* GILBERT *appears with the girl from the teahouse at the Japanese Exhibition. They are followed by* BARKER, *two other Japanese ladies (the dancer and the singer) and a Japanese* GENTLEMAN. *The ladies are all in Japanese street-wear, but the gentleman sports a top hat. Also present are* LEONORA, JESSIE *and* SIBYL, HELEN *and* CELLIER, *who takes his position at a conductor's stand on the platform, and several other actors and actresses. These include* LELY, *who stands on the side of the stage, and* TEMPLE, BARRINGTON *and* BOVILL, *who drift into the stalls with a few gentlemen choristers. The accompanist,* MRS RUSSELL, *takes her place at the upright piano at the side of the stage.* GILBERT *and* BARKER *wear their top hats. Hats are worn by all the women present except the Japanese.*

GILBERT: Thank you, Seymour.

SEYMOUR: Sir.

GILBERT: Now, Miss Sixpence-Please, could you kindly come along with me?

BARKER: Make haste! Make haste! (*To* D'AUBAN) Johnny!

GILBERT: Thank you very much.

(MISS SIXPENCE-PLEASE *has sat down.* BARKER *taps on the floor with his cane.*)

BARKER: Please take a seat now.

GILBERT: Ladies and gentlemen, I'd just like to introduce you all to Miss Sixpence-Please, a young lady of whom some of you will have heard me speak with reverence and respect. Thank you.

(*During this,* SEYMOUR *has put out more chairs, whilst the other two Japanese ladies are entertained by* D'AUBAN, *who greets them with stage 'Chinese' bows.*)

Kindly make yourselves comfortable. Please be seated. Thank you.

(*The* JAPANESE LADIES *join* MISS SIXPENCE-PLEASE. GILBERT *addresses the* JAPANESE GENTLEMAN.)

Ah, sir! My apologies – I've been neglecting you. Would you like to come this way?

(GILBERT *conducts him to a high chair on the platform.* SEYMOUR *points to another chair.*)

No, it's alright, Seymour, he can use your chair. Far more appropriate. Here you are, sir – be seated here. Very good indeed. Pride of place, sir. Make yourself comfortable. Cellier! Yes. Now.

(D'AUBAN *is now centre stage, giving his impression of a comic rooster.*)

D'Auban! Will you kindly withdraw to the side of the stage immediately?!

BARKER: Johnny!

HELEN: Thank you, Monsieur D'Auban.

(D'AUBAN *ceases.*)

CELLIER: Ladies, will you take up your fans, please?

(LEONORA, JESSIE *and* SIBYL *assemble upstage.*)

GILBERT (*to the* GENTLEMAN): What I'd like you to do, sir, is to observe the proceedings. (*To the* LADIES:) Would you kindly give all your attention to the performance? Thank you.
(BARKER *has drifted centre stage.*)
Barker, what are you doing? Do you propose to join in?
BARKER: My dancing days are long over, Mr Gilbert.
(*He does a tiny dance-step, and withdraws. In the stalls,* BARRINGTON *guffaws.*)
GILBERT: Over, Barker, but not forgotten!
D'AUBAN (*Cockney/theatrical*): Ladies . . . opening attitudes, *s'il vous plaît*.
CELLIER: From the beginning of the song, counting two bars before, Mrs Russell.
MRS RUSSELL: Thank you.
CELLIER (*baton in hand*): One, two – two, two.
(MRS RUSSELL *plays the introduction to the song; the three actresses perform it side-by-side in a row. Their gestures are very much in the pantomime 'Chinky Chinese' mode.* D'AUBAN *monitors their performance alongside them. They advance downstage until they are right on top of their three counterparts, who are a little nonplussed.*)
ALL THREE (*sing*):
Three little maids from school are we,
Pert as a schoolgirl well can be,
Fill'd to the brim with girlish glee,
Three little maids from school!
D'AUBAN: Fans!
(GROSSMITH *arrives with a newspaper.*)
LEONORA (*sings*):
Everything is a source of fun.
(*They all do comic 'oriental' side-to-side head movements;* D'AUBAN *joins in.*)
SIBYL (*sings*):
Nobody's safe, for we care for none!
(*They turn upstage and do funny 'tail' gestures with their fans. This amuses the two other* LADIES, *but not* MISS SIXPENCE-PLEASE.)

JESSIE (*sings*):
>Life is a joke that's just begun!
>(D'OYLY CARTE *arrives, and crosses the stage to the platform.*)

ALL THREE (*sing*):
>Three little maids from school!

D'AUBAN: Fans rising slowly. And – !

ALL THREE (*sing*):
>Three little maids who, all unwary,
>Come from a ladies' seminary –
>(*They do a sort of 'negro serenader' cakewalk.*)

GILBERT: Stop. Thank you very much. Now, Miss Sixpence-Please – Carte!

CARTE: Gilbert.

GILBERT: I beg your pardon. Let me introduce our Japanese guests.

CARTE (*doffing his hat*): Ladies.

GILBERT: Mr D'Oyly Carte, our proprietor.
(*The* GENTLEMAN *removes his top hat self-consciously.*)

CARTE: Please continue.

GILBERT: Thank you very much. Now, Miss Sixpence-Please: that performance that you have just witnessed was not even remotely Japanese. Am I right? Japanese!
(MISS SIXPENCE-PLEASE *is stuck. She whispers to the* JAPANESE GENTLEMAN.)
Sir. Japanese?

GENTLEMAN: Japanese.

GILBERT: No!

GENTLEMAN: No.

GILBERT: Thank you very much.

D'AUBAN: Excuse me, Mr Gilbert, sir, if I may. (*To* GENTLEMAN:) Japanese?

GENTLEMAN: Japanese.

D'AUBAN: Yes.

GENTLEMAN: Yes.

D'AUBAN: You see, he hasn't got the faintest idea what you're talking about.
(*Loud mirth from* BARRINGTON *and others in the stalls.*)

GILBERT: Well, that's blatantly obvious, D'Auban!

MRS RUSSELL (*London Italian*): *Allora*, er, *parlate italiano*?

GILBERT (*shouting*): If he doesn't speak English, he's hardly likely to speak Italian, is he, Mrs Russell? – For goodness' sake!!!
MRS RUSSELL: I beg your pardon, Mr Gilbert, but – *Porca miseria! Ma non posso lavorare così.*
CELLIER: Mrs Russell!!
MRS RUSSELL: It's a waste of time!
CELLIER (*silencing her*): Ah!
GILBERT: Now, if you three ladies would like to come with me. (*He strides purposefully upstage.*)
SEYMOUR: Please go to the back of the stage . . . thank you!
BARKER: Yes, yes. Come upstage! As quickly as you can – come along! Come along!
SEYMOUR: Thank you!
(BARKER *taps his cane on the stage.*)
Thank you.
(*The three* JAPANESE LADIES *join* GILBERT *upstage by the back-cloth, where he places them in position.*)
GILBERT: Thank you. Thank you . . . very much indeed – one; two; three. Very good. Thank you. Now, what I would like you to do, when the music commences, I would like you to advance downstage. Thank you very much. Cellier.
CELLIER: One, two – two, two.
(MRS RUSSELL *plays the introduction. The* LADIES *don't move.*)
GILBERT: Off you go. Come along. Come on . . . Stop. Stop. Stop.
CELLIER: Thank you, Mrs Russell.
(*The music stops.*)
D'AUBAN: Will this take long? I'm to arrange a mazurka at four o'clock.
GILBERT: It is apparent that I have not made myself clear. Now, when Mrs Russell commences playing on the pianoforte – diddle-dum, diddle-dee, diddle-dee, diddle-dee – what I would like you to do is to advance downstage, *comme ça*: diddle-dum, diddle-doo, diddle-dee, diddle-dee. (*He accompanies this rendering with a whimsical walk. Loud mirth from the stalls.*)
You understand?

(*Two of the* LADIES *confer.*)
I think you do. Let's try once more. Cellier.
CELLIER: One, two – two, two.
(MRS RUSSELL *plays. The three* LADIES *walk downstage.* MISS SIXPENCE-PLEASE *remains impassive, but the other two display coy charm.* GILBERT *walks alongside them, shouting encouragement.*)
GILBERT: Come along, come along! That's it. Very good! Excellent. That is exactly it. Thank you very much indeed. Excellent! First rate! Thank you very much indeed! Good! (*The music peters out. The three* LADIES *stand about with* JESSIE, SIBYL *and others.*)
Now, D'Auban. That is exactly what I want.
D'AUBAN: I do beg your pardon, Mr Gilbert, but I appear to have missed the point somewhat.
GILBERT: That is the very effect I need.
D'AUBAN: And what effect exactly is that?
GILBERT: Did you not see what they did?
D'AUBAN: Yes, they walked downstage.
BARKER: They appeared to me to be ambling along the Strand.
JESSIE: Simply walking.
GILBERT: They walked downstage in the Japanese manner.
D'AUBAN: They walked downstage in the Japanese manner because they are Japanese.
GILBERT: Exactly; and that is precisely why they are here.
D'AUBAN: Our three little maids are not Japanese – however, they are very funny.
GILBERT: No funnier, however, than they would be if they all sat down on pork pies.
(*Loud mirth from all.*)
D'AUBAN: Young feller-me-lad, Mr Gilbert, sir. I've arranged terpischore – Chinese, Japanese, everybody-wash-your-knees – for pantomime, burlesque and the ballet, for many a season, always to great acclaim.
GILBERT: D'Auban, this is not low burlesque, this is an entirely original Japanese opera. Now, Miss Bond, Miss Braham and Miss Grey – kindly resume your opening positions.
(JESSIE *and* SIBYL *march upstage.*)
Please be seated once more, thank you. Please be seated.

SEYMOUR: Thank you.
(*The three Japanese* LADIES *sit down.*)
GILBERT (to LEONORA): Come along, Tortoise – quickly, quickly!
(LEONORA *languidly joins the others.*)
What I would like you to do now is to perform it just as you have seen our guests perform it. Thank you very much.
JESSIE: Mr Gilbert.
GILBERT: Yes, Jessie?
JESSIE: Would that be exactly as we have just seen demonstrated?
GILBERT: Exactly.
SIBYL: Without using Monsieur D'Auban's steps, Mr Gilbert?
GILBERT: I want you to perform it precisely as you have seen our Japanese friends perform it. Thank you very much!
LEONORA: *Exactement – c'est pas difficile.*
D'AUBAN: In other words, wery slowly and wery boringly.
CELLIER: One, two – two, two.
(MRS RUSSELL *plays the introduction. The three actresses proceed slowly downstage, imitating the coy behaviour of their guests.*)

GILBERT: Very good. First rate. That is exactly right – thank you very much indeed.
CELLIER: Thank you, Mrs Russell . . .
(*The music stops.*)
D'AUBAN: I haven't laughed so much since me tights caught fire in *Harlequin Meets Itchity-Switch in the Nitch!*
SEYMOUR: Decorum in rehearsal, Monsieur D'Auban!

A little later on the stage. The three actresses face their guests, who are showing them how to use their fans. GILBERT *and* D'AUBAN *are close by, watching. So is* LELY. *Much shared laughter and goodwill.*
GILBERT: That's the way – yes! Very good indeed.
D'AUBAN: Try it altogether – try it altogether.
GILBERT: Try it . . .
D'AUBAN: Try together.
GILBERT: Three of them, do it together. The same noise.
GILBERT AND D'AUBAN (*together*): One, two, three –
(*The actresses flick their fans vigorously in unison. Everybody laughs.*)
GILBERT: Ah! Excellent!
(*The Japanese* DANCER *flicks her fan.*)

Another 'flash-forward'. The same song in performance on the Savoy stage. The coy Japanese behaviour now informs the playing style. The staging is symmetrical. LEONORA, JESSIE *and* SIBYL *break through the semicircle of the Ladies' chorus, which then divides into two lines as the Three Little Maids take centre stage. Elaborate fan business throughout.*
ALL THREE (*sing*):
    Three little maids from school are we,
    Pert as a schoolgirl well can be,
    Fill'd to the brim with girlish glee,
    Three little maids from school!
LEONORA (*sings*):
    Everything is a source of fun.
    (*Mock whisper to* JESSIE, *who giggles with glee.*)
SIBYL (*sings*):
    Nobody's safe for we care for none!
    (*Eavesdropping 'attitude' from one half of the chorus.*)

JESSIE (*sings*):
>Life is a joke that's just begun!
>(*Mock shock from the other half.*)

ALL THREE (*singing and bowing*):
>Three little maids from school!
>Three little maids who, all unwary,
>Come from a ladies' seminary,
>Freed from its genius tutelary –
>Three little maids from school.
>Three little maids from school.

LEONORA (*sings*):
>One little maid is a bride, Yum-Yum –

SIBYL (*sings*):
>Two little maids in attendance come –

JESSIE (*sings*):
>Three little maids is the total sum.

ALL (*sing*):
>Three little maids from school!

LEONORA (*sings*):
>From three little maids take one away –

SIBYL (*sings*):
>Two little maids remain, and they –

JESSIE (*sings*):
>Won't have to wait very long, they say –

ALL THREE (*singing and bowing*):
>Three little maids from school!

CHORUS (*sings*):
>Three little maids from school!

EVERYBODY (*sings*):
>Three little maids who, all unwary,
>Come from a ladies' seminary,
>Freed from its genius tutelary –

ALL THREE (*sing*):
>Three little maids from school –

EVERYBODY (*sings*):
>Three little maids from school!
>(*Dance routine; the three actresses end in the famous pose.*)

GILBERT *is at work in his study. Night. On the desk is a model theatre containing the set for Act 2 of* The Mikado – *Ko-Ko's garden. Using an army of little coloured striped blocks,* GILBERT *is plotting the characters' moves. He shunts them around, reciting each part – he knows all the lines.*

GILBERT (*reciting*):
>Laughing, Ha! ha!
>Chaffing, Ha! ha!
>Nectar quaffing, Ha! ha! ha!
>But condemned to die is he,
>Wretched, meritorious B!

(*To himself.*)
>The Mikado leads Katisha off . . .

(*He 'walks' two of the blocks off the stage.*)

A functional rehearsal room somewhere in London. Day. A little stage at one end; a rehearsal table at the other. GILBERT *is on stage with* GROSSMITH, JESSIE *and* BARRINGTON, *who are fully clad in their street-wear, hats included.* GILBERT *is wearing his hat, and is demonstrating a piece of fan business: he is holding a fan with one end touching the tip of his nose, as in 'cocking a snook'.*

GILBERT: Thus.

(*Laughter.*)

>The traditional Japanese posture, as adopted by well-meaning but misguided underlings upon the departure of their august superiors. Thank you.

(*He gives the fan to* BARRINGTON, *and leaves the stage.*)

GROSSMITH: Would that be a recognized Japanese attitude, sir?

GILBERT: Not as yet, Grossmith, but I have every confidence that it will become one.

(*He stands by the rehearsal table.* SEYMOUR, *also in hat and coat, gives* GROSSMITH *a fan.*)

GROSSMITH: Much obliged. I'm sure I've seen this on a vase somewhere.

(BARRINGTON *laughs. All three actors adopt the pose, fans to their noses.*)

GILBERT: Jessie . . .

(*He goes to the stage, and adjusts her fan.*)

JESSIE: Thank you, Mr Gilbert.

(GILBERT *surveys the trio.* SEYMOUR *sits at the table with the prompt-book.*)

GILBERT: Ha! Pretty picture. Eh, Seymour?

SEYMOUR: Charming, sir.

GILBERT: The Mikado has left. Grossmith.
(*They drop their fans.*)

GROSSMITH: Well, another fine mess you've got us into –
(GILBERT *goes on to the stage.*)

GILBERT: No, Grossmith. My line is, 'A nice mess you've got us into' –
(*He takes* GROSSMITH'*s fan.*)

GROSSMITH: Nice mess . . .

GILBERT: – and I should be much obliged if you would play it *comme ça*: 'Well' (*He closes the fan sharply.*) 'a nice mess you've got us into.' (*He moves between* BARRINGTON *and* JESSIE.)

GROSSMITH: (*taking fan*): Righto, sir.
(GILBERT *returns to the table. In what follows,* GROSSMITH *snaps the fan shut before the 'well' rather than after it.*)
(*Snap*) Well –

GILBERT: No: well. (*Claps hands.*)

GROSSMITH: Well, (*snap, move*) a nice mess you've got us into, with your nodding head and the deference due to a man of pedigree!

GILBERT: Mr Grossmith, you are under sentence of death, by something lingering. Either boiling oil or melted lead. Kindly bear that in mind. Thank you.

GROSSMITH (*'nervous'*): Well, a nice mess you've got us into, with your nodding head and the deference due to a man of pedigree!

BARRINGTON: Merely corroborative detail, intended to give artistic verisimilitude to a bald and unconvincing narrative.

GILBERT: No, Barrington. An otherwise bald and unconvincing narrative.

BARRINGTON: Was that incorrect? I – I do beg your pardon.

GILBERT: No, sir. It has only just occurred to me.

BARRINGTON: To an otherwise bald and unconvincing narrative.

GILBERT: Much better.

JESSIE: Corrobotative detail indeed!
GILBERT: *Corroborative* detail.
JESSIE: Corrobotative.
  (GILBERT *comes very close to* JESSIE, *face-to-face*.)
GILBERT: Corroborative.
JESSIE: Corroborative.
GILBERT: Corroborative.
JESSIE: Corroborative.
  (GILBERT *returns to the table*.)
GILBERT: Thank you. Splendid.
JESSIE: Corroborative detail indeed! Corroborative fiddlestick!
GROSSMITH: And you're just as bad as he is with your cock-and-bull stories.
SEYMOUR: Cock-and-*a*-bull.
GROSSMITH: Cock-and-*a*-bull; about catching his eye . . . Line?
GILBERT/SEYMOUR (*together*): And his whistling an air.
GROSSMITH: And his whistling hair.
  (*All three actors laugh uproariously*.)
GILBERT: Boiling oil, Grossmith, melted lead.
GROSSMITH: Beg pardon, sir. About catching his eye, and his whistling an air. But that's so like you! You must stick your oar in!
SEYMOUR: You must *put in* your oar.
GILBERT: Over again.
GROSSMITH: And you're just as bad as he is, with your cock-and-a-bull stories about catching his eye, and his whistling an air. But that's so like you! You must put your oar in!
SEYMOUR: You must *put in* your oar.
GILBERT: Over again.
GROSSMITH: And you're just as bad as he is, with your cock-and-a-bull stories about catching his eye, and his whistling an air. But that's so like you! You must put in your oar!
BARRINGTON: Yes, but how about your big right arm?
JESSIE: Yes, and your snickersnee!
GROSSMITH: Well, well, never mind that now. There's only one thing to be done. Nanki-Poo hasn't started yet – he must come to life again – at once!
  (*Pause*. GILBERT *looks reflective*.)
Appear, appear, appear!

(*They all laugh.*)

GILBERT: Yes . . . now since Nanki-Poo and Yum-Yum have decided not to grace us with their presence, it would transpire, Mr Seymour, that your moment of glory has finally arrived.
(SEYMOUR *laughs politely and attends to the prompt-book.*)
On yer feet, Slopkins!!
(*The actors all explode with laughter. So does* GILBERT. SEYMOUR, *not the least amused, proceeds to the stage with the book.*)

SEYMOUR: Whence would you like us both to enter, sir?
(GILBERT *goes on stage to demonstrate.*)

GILBERT: The honeymoon couple appear at the upstage-right entrance, travelling in a westerly direction towards Knightsbridge. But your journey is interrupted by Mr Grossmith.

JESSIE: Mr Gilbert?

GILBERT: Jessie.

JESSIE: Might I use my stick?

GILBERT (*quietly*): By all means. Are you troubled?

JESSIE (*quietly*): I'm quite alright, thank you.
(GILBERT *returns to the table.*)

GROSSMITH: Well, well?

GILBERT: Well, well.

GROSSMITH: Well, well, never mind that now. There's only one thing to be done. Nanki-Poo hasn't started yet – he must come to life again – at once.
(SEYMOUR *crosses the back of the stage, doing a funny walk.*)
Here he comes. 'Ere, Nanki-Poo.
(SEYMOUR *joins the others.*)
I've good news for yer. You're reprieved.
(SEYMOUR *places an imaginary object on the floor.*)

SEYMOUR: I beg your pardon, Mr Gilbert . . . I have failed to provide a valise.

GILBERT: Indeed, Seymour, and you have also failed to provide two actors. Pray continue.

SEYMOUR (*over-acting*): Oh, but it's too late!
(BARRINGTON *roars with laughter.*)
I'm a dead man, and I'm off for my honeymoon.

GROSSMITH: Uncanny, is it not?
GILBERT: Mr Seymour, please inform Mr Lely that his services will no longer be required.
(JESSIE *giggles*.)
SEYMOUR (*seriously*): Thank you very much, sir.
GROSSMITH: Nonsense. A terrible thing 'as 'appened. It seems you're the son o' the Mikado.
GILBERT: A terrible thing has just happened, Grossmith – you've become a cockney!
GROSSMITH: I thought one would suggest something of his lowly station, being a cheap tailor and all.
GILBERT: Rubbish – we're in Japan, for heaven's sake, not Stepney or Bow. Do it properly!
GROSSMITH: Oh, very well. Nonsense. A terrible thing has happened. It seems you're the son of the Mikado.
SEYMOUR: Yes, but that happened some time ago.
GROSSMITH: Is this a time for airy persiflidge?
GILBERT: Pers*iflage*, Grossmith.
GROSSMITH: Is it?
GILBERT: It is.
GROSSMITH: Is this a time for airy persiflage? Doesn't sound right to me.
GILBERT: Persiflage, mirage, *fromage*.
BARRINGTON: *Découpage*.
GILBERT: Exactly.
GROSSMITH: Your father is here, and with Ka-*tisha*!
GILBERT: Katisha.
GROSSMITH: It amuses me to say 'Ka-tisha'.
GILBERT: It doesn't amuse me, Grossmith. Nor does it scan.
SEYMOUR: My father! And with Katisha!
GROSSMITH: Yes, he wants you particularly.
BARRINGTON: So does she.
(SEYMOUR *touches his hat to* JESSIE, *who makes room for him to take* LEONORA's *part*.)
SEYMOUR (*as Yum-Yum*): Oh, but he's married now.
(*The others giggle*.)
GROSSMITH: But bless my heart! What has that to do with it?
SEYMOUR (*as Nanki-Poo*): Katisha claims me in marriage, but I can't marry her because I'm married already.

Consequently she will insist on my execution and if I'm executed, my wife will have to be buried alive.

SEYMOUR (*as Yum-Yum*): You see our difficulty.

GROSSMITH: Yes. I don't know what's to be done.

GILBERT (to GROSSMITH): Make as to leave. (to SEYMOUR) Stop him.

SEYMOUR (*as Nanki-Poo*): There's one chance for you. If you could persuade Katisha to marry you, she would have no further claim on me, and in that case I could come to life without any fear of being put to death.

GROSSMITH: I . . . marry . . . Katisha?

SEYMOUR (*as Yum-Yum*): I really think it's the only course.

GROSSMITH: My good girl, have you seen 'er? She's something awful.

SEYMOUR: Appalling.

GROSSMITH: Something appalling.

JESSIE: Ah, that's only her face.

(GILBERT *guides* JESSIE *to another position.*)

Ah, that's only her face. She has a left elbow which people come miles to see.

BARRINGTON (*slurred*): I am told her right heel is much admired by connoisseurs.

GILBERT: Could we do that line again, please, Barrington, and this time try it in English?

BARRINGTON (*clearer*): I'm told her right heel is much admired by connoisseurs. That better, sir?

GILBERT: Marginally.

GROSSMITH: My good sir . . . I decline to pin my heart on any lady's right heel.

GILBERT (to GROSSMITH): Make as to leave. (to SEYMOUR) Stop him.

SEYMOUR: It comes to this: while Katisha is single, I prefer to be a disembodied spirit. When Katisha is married, existence will be as welcome as the flowers in spring.

GROSSMITH: Tra-la.

(*Somewhere near by, a train whistles as it pulls out of a station.*)

GILBERT: Very good. Over again, if you please.

At the Savoy. SULLIVAN *is conducting his band. Behind him is the empty auditorium.* CELLIER *stands beside him.* LOUIS *sits alone in the stalls. They are rehearsing the beginning of the* Mikado *overture. After a few bars,* SULLIVAN *shouts, 'And – !' He sings along a little, and when the playing is a touch out,* CELLIER *grins at him and he puffs a bit, but with a twinkle. After the first section, he stops, puts down his baton, and removes his monocle.*

SULLIVAN: Thank you, gentlemen. Not surprisingly, we were somewhat foxed by the abbreviated, er – restatement. Discord bordering on cacophony . . . Second fiddles?

1ST VIOLINIST: Indeed, Sir Arthur.

2ND VIOLINIST: My mistake, Sir Arthur. I do beg your pardon. My error, sir.

SULLIVAN: I suspect you were, Mr Harris and more than a trifle. I really don't mind whose mistake – (*He coughs;* CELLIER *looks concerned.*)
– it was, Mr Plank, as long as it doesn't happen again. The entry is on the third beat of the bar, not the first. I think that's quite clear.

HARRIS (*1st*): Yes, sir.

PLANK (*2nd*): It is, sir, yes.

SULLIVAN: Very good. And now . . . we return to Mr Hurley. Good morning, Mr Hurley.
(MR HURLEY, *the bassoonist, is a middle-aged man with the look of a mad professor.*)

HURLEY: Good morning, Dr Sullivan.

SULLIVAN (*cockney accent*): You was late, Mr 'Urley.
(*Everybody laughs – except* MR HURLEY.)

HURLEY: My profuse apologies to you, sir.

SULLIVAN: Thank you.

HURLEY: I assume it to be an error on the part of the copyist. Er, the second beat of the previous bar appeared to me to be masquerading as the first beat of the next.

SULLIVAN: Most alarming. But it was not?

HURLEY: Oh, indeed not – for which I do apologize, Dr Sullivan.

CELLIER: Mr Hurley, once again (to SULLIVAN) – saving your blushes, maestro – (*to* HURLEY) Dr Sullivan is dead. Long live Sir Arthur.

(HURLEY *does not look pleased.*)
SULLIVAN: Thank you, Mr Cellier. Mr Tripp.
TRIPP: Sir!
   (TRIPP *is the percussionist – short, tough, dapper, moustache, bowler hat, shirtsleeves.*)
SULLIVAN: Owing to the somewhat tardy entry of Mr Hurley, you, quite understandably, followed suit.
TRIPP: Absolutely, sir.
SULLIVAN: So assuming that Mr Hurley does enter at the correct place, you will too?
TRIPP: Assuming he does, sir, I will, sir.
SULLIVAN: Very good. Thank you, Mr Tripp.
TRIPP: Thank you, sir.
   (TRIPP *and* HURLEY *exchange hostile looks.*)
SULLIVAN: Capital. Er, gentlemen, once more from the beginning, please. I shall give you one bar.

The dress rehearsal of The Mikado. TEMPLE *is on stage with the* CHORUS. *Full costumes, wigs, make-up. The Act 2 set is fully lit.* SULLIVAN *is conducting the band in his shirtsleeves.* CELLIER *sits near him. Scattered around the stalls are* GILBERT *and various members of the Savoy team.* GILBERT *is smoking a cigar, and looks fed up.* WILHELM *is expressionless.* D'AUBAN, *puffing on his pipe, mimes the song* TEMPLE *is performing, and silently performs his actions;* CARTE *and* HELEN *are thoroughly enjoying themselves, and are much amused, as is* CELLIER. MADAME LEON *smiles occasionally, but her assistants look characteristically worried; and* BARKER *sits at a large table and smokes a cigarette. At the back of the stalls, a few other unidentified folk watch discreetly – men in hats, mostly; one woman.*

SULLIVAN *conducts the opening bars as* TEMPLE, *resplendent as the Mikado, strides down the steps.*
TEMPLE (*sings*):
   A more humane Mikado never
   Did in Japan exist.
   To nobody second
   I'm certainly reckon'd
   A true philanthropist.

It is my very humane endeavour
To make, to some extent,
Each evil liver
A running river
Of harmless merriment.
(*During the following, the ladies' and gentlemen's* CHORUS
perform fan movements in unison.)
My object all sublime
I shall achieve in time –
To let the punishment fit the crime –
The punishment fit the crime;
And make each pris'ner pent
Unwillingly represent
A source of innocent merriment!
Of innocent merriment!
(GILBERT *stubs out his cigar in* BARKER'*s ashtray, sips some
water from a glass, and sits down glumly in a seat.*)
The advertising quack who wearies
With tales of countless cures,
His teeth, I've enacted,
Shall all be extracted
By terrified amateurs.
The music hall singer attends a series
Of masses and fugues and 'ops'
By Bach, interwoven
With Spohr and Beethoven
At classical Monday pops.

The billiard sharp whom anyone catches
His doom's extremely hard –
He's made to dwell
In a dungeon cell
On a spot that's always barred.
And there he plays extravagant matches
In fitless finger stalls
On a cloth untrue,
With a twisted cue
And elliptical billiard balls!

>   My object all sublime
>   I shall achieve in time –
>   To let the punishment fit the crime –
>   The punishment fit the crime;
>   And make each pris'ner pent
>   Unwillingly represent
>   A source of innocent merriment!
>   Of innocent merriment!
>   (GILBERT *makes a note in a pocket-book. During the following,* TEMPLE, *revealing white stockings, performs a comic dance. This much amuses* HELEN *and* MADAME LEON, *but* GILBERT *remains gloomy.*)

CHORUS (*sings*):
>   His object all sublime
>   He will achieve in time –
>   To let the punishment fit the crime –
>   The punishment fit the crime;
>   And make each pris'ner pent
>   Unwillingly represent
>   A source of innocent merriment!
>   Of innocent merriment!
>   (*At the end of his dance,* TEMPLE *opens his huge fan and freezes in a comic attitude.*)

SEYMOUR *knocks on a door and tries to open it, but it is locked. A voice from within* . . .
GROSSMITH: Did I say, 'Come in'?
SEYMOUR: You are required in the auditorium, Mr Grossmith.

It is GROSSMITH'S *dressing-room. He reclines on an ottoman, mopping his brow with a silk cloth. He is wearing his Ko-Ko wig and make-up, and his costume.* COOK, *his dresser, waits with him in the room.*
GROSSMITH (*frail voice*): I requested five minutes' grace.
SEYMOUR: You have had eight, sir.
   (*Pause.*)
GROSSMITH: Mayn't it wait until tomorrow?
SEYMOUR: No, sir.
   (GROSSMITH *sighs, and covers his face with the cloth.*)

In the auditorium. Minutes later. The orchestra pit is empty. In front of the closed curtain GILBERT, SULLIVAN, CARTE, CELLIER, WILHELM *and* HELEN *stand in an informal line across the front of the stalls.* D'AUBAN *dances to himself in a side aisle.* BARKER *is still at his table. The whole cast is assembled in the seats, the principals to the front, the* CHORUS *behind.* LEONORA *appears at a door. She looks flushed and unfocused.* GROSSMITH *follows, now without his wig but with his costume and make-up, and wearing his pince-nez. He looks unwell.* SEYMOUR *follows them both. All the actors are wearing some make-up and costume.*

GILBERT: Thank you, Miss Braham. Is that everyone, Seymour?

SEYMOUR: All present and correct, Mr Gilbert.

GILBERT: Good.
(LEONORA *sits next to* LELY, *who attends to her folding seat.*)
I won't keep you, ladies and gentlemen. I know we're all extremely tired, and looking forward to getting home to our yawning beds.
(*Various people laugh, including* TEMPLE, *who is in the front row.*)
Observations. The use of fans, particularly in Act One, was flabby and erratic.

D'AUBAN: Wery scrappy.

GILBERT: Indeed, D'Auban. We shall address this tomorrow afternoon at two o'clock, Seymour.

SEYMOUR: Two of the clock. (*He makes a note.*)

GILBERT: Ko-Ko's entrance. Mr Kent and Mr Conyngham. Please ensure that you do not flinch at Mr Grossmith's sword. You must have confidence that he is not about to chop off your heads. Even if it may appear that that is your inevitable fate.
(*General mirth.* TEMPLE *chuckles.*)
I take it, Mr Grossmith, that this evening's performance was an aberration. (*Pause*). Grossmith!
(GROSSMITH *is half-concealed behind a column. He is still mopping his face.*)

GROSSMITH: I beg your pardon, sir. Were you addressing me?

GILBERT: I was indeed, sir. How are you?

GROSSMITH: Quite well, thank you. I believe a good night's sleep will cure all ills.

GILBERT: That I took to be the case. (*To everybody*) your performances were, on the whole, promising, which is more than can be said, alas, for that of the sliding doors . . .

(*Laughter.*)

. . . one of which might have thought it was in Japan, but the other was apparently stubbornly labouring under the misapprehension that it was on holiday in Yorkshire.

(*Loud mirth, not least from* TEMPLE.)

Where was the man, Mr Seymour?

SEYMOUR: Rest assured, Mr Barker, that tomorrow night he will be with us in Japan.

GILBERT: Capital. Now. Cuts. There is only one. In Act Two: the Mikado's 'Song'.

(*Pause. Obvious universal shock and surprise. Murmurs. Then an actress in the fourth row speaks. She is* ROSINA BRANDRAM, *who plays Katisha.*)

ROSINA: I beg your pardon, Mr Gilbert.

GILBERT: Yes, Miss Brandram?

ROSINA: Surely, you can't mean Mr Temple's solo?

GILBERT: That is exactly what I mean.

(*Pause.*)

ROSINA: I do think that's a shame, sir.

JESSIE: It's a dreadful shame.

BARRINGTON: Hear, hear.

(*A few people murmur. Pause.* TEMPLE *clears his throat*).

TEMPLE: My . . . my, my dear Mr Gilbert . . .

GILBERT: Temple?

TEMPLE: I am fully aware that the standard of my singing was not quite up to the mark . . .

GILBERT: Your singing was exemplary, Temple.

TEMPLE: But I – I can assure you that once I have mastered the leg business, I shall most certainly be at liberty to serve the lyric.

GILBERT: I do apologize, Temple – I've not made myself clear. My decision to cut the song in no way reflects upon your performance of it, which was fine in every respect.

SULLIVAN: Hear, hear.
GILBERT: The fault, if there is one, lies in my obtuse decision to write the thing in the first place. I have nothing more to say. Thank you very much. Sullivan . . .
TEMPLE: Excuse me.
(*He gets up and leaves. After a few moments,* SEYMOUR *follows him.* SULLIVAN *watches them, cigarette-holder in hand. Then:*)
SULLIVAN: Ladies and gentlemen . . . er, if I might presume to take a few more moments of your time, I should like to thank you all most passionately for your tremendous hard work and application during these last few weeks. And, if I may say so, the contribution of the chorus was particularly fine.
CELLIER: Hear, hear.
SULLIVAN: I am immensely proud of you all. I do not wish to tempt the fates, but I feel that we will have a great success. I have nothing further to add. Only remember . . . '*voce, voce, voce*'.
(*Comfortable laughter.*)
Buona notte a tutti.
(CARTE *steps forward to speak, but* D'AUBAN *beats him to it.*)
D'AUBAN (*pipe in mouth*): Now then, young feller-me-lads. On the whole the terpischore was executed wery magnifiquely, notwithstanding the, er, topsy-turvydom befuddling Mr Ko-Ko's entrance. Otherwise, 'in the sea, in the sea, in the sea, in the sea': fans out on 'sea' – not in. (*He puts on his top hat.*) Er, should any gent require a libation, I shall shortly be located at the 'Coal Hole' with Mr Johnny Ward.
(*Laughter.* D'AUBAN *picks up a carpet-bag and leaves. Music cue 14 starts.*)
CARTE: Thank you, Johnny. (*To everybody*) Excellent. *Bravissimi*. A splendid achievement. Be confident; and . . . may you have a good night's rest. Miss Lenoir.
HELEN: My thanks and congratulations to you all. Now to hasten you to your slumbers, cabs have been ordered and will meet you at the stage door as soon as you are ready. Thank you.
BARKER: Yes . . . and please share a cab with a neighbour. Remember, we are not made of money.

SEYMOUR: Thank you, ladies and gentlemen.
>   (GILBERT *watches the company get up and file out. Music cue 14 ends as the next scene begins.*)

A few minutes later. In the Ladies' CHORUS dressing-room. Various stages of dress.
MISS BARNES (*in underwear; sad*): I felt so terrible.
MISS WARREN (*ready to leave; jaunty hat*): Oh, so did I.
MISS BARNES: My heart broke for him – I can't bear to see a man cry.
MISS BROWN (*underwear; wiping off make-up*): Was he crying?
MISS MOORE (*off*): He was crushed.
MISS WILLIAMSON (*wholesome; dressed to go*): Really sad.
MISS WARREN: And he's so awfully funny.
MISS BARNES: And there's people 'oo only come to see Mr Temple perform.
MISS BETTS (*fastening corset*): I agree.
MISS CARLISLE (*underwear; lacing a boot*): My cousins are always askin' about him. They've already purchased their tickets.
MISS BROWN: They'll – they'll want their money back now. (*She giggles.*)
MISS JARDINE (*small; fully dressed; severe*): There are other people in this piece apart from Mr Temple, don't you know.
MISS MEADOWS (*underwear*): Yes, well he's hardly in it now though, is he, Rose?
MISS RUSSELL (*ready to leave; indignant*): He's playing the Mikado!
MISS MEADOWS: Thank you, Violet!
MISS TRINGHAM (*sitting waiting; dressed*): Oh, come along, Ellen – be quick!
MISS JARDINE: Will you be long, Catherine?
MISS BETTS (*irritable*): No, I shan't!
MISS CARLISLE: I wish there was something we could do.
MISS JARDINE (*putting on gloves*): Well, there ain't – Mr Gilbert's made his decision, and that's that.
MISS KINGSLEY (*plump; dressed*): With Mr Gilbert one never really knows, particularly before a first night.

MISS LANGTON-JAMES (*blonde; dressed*): I suggest we all go home and get a good night's sleep
MISS RUSSELL (*bossy; incensed; leaving*): Absolutely. I'm certainly off. I think you should all button your lips and mind your own business. Goodnight!
(*She storms out. General laughter and chatter. Then* MISS WARREN *in a cheerful jaunty hat, proceeds to leave* . . .)
MISS WARREN: Goodnight, girls. I don't want to be late for supper.
MISS JARDINE: Catherine, I'll wait for you downstairs. (*She leaves.*)
MISS KINGSLEY (*to* MISS WARREN): Oh, Bunny – you look charming!
MISS BETTS (*to* MISS JARDINE): I'll be along in a jiffy.

Meanwhile in the dressing-room of the Gentlemen's CHORUS. *Again, various states of readiness. No beards, sideburns or moustaches.*
EVANS (*Northern; fastening tie*): It's a fine comic song.
FLAGSTONE (*Northern; shirtsleeves*): It is.
EVANS: He sings it splendidly –
FLAGSTONE: He does.
EVANS: And do you not conceive, gentlemen, that the paying audience deserves to hear it?
SEVERAL PEOPLE: Yes.
FLAGSTONE: I agree, Walter. They do.
CONYNGHAM (*tall; long hair*): Rotten luck for poor old Temple.
LEWIS (*dapper; fastening tie*): I'm not convinced it's as immortal a song as all that.
FLAGSTONE: Nobody said the song was immortal, Mr Lewis.
LEWIS: Well, you're discussing it as though it were the Holy Grail.
EVANS: Notwithstanding your reservation about the song, Lewis, you must concede that it is a highly original performance.
LEWIS: He'd have done better to have cut one of Grossmith's songs.
RHYS (*Welsh; small*): Mr Grossmith is a little poorly, Mr Lewis.
LEWIS: Well, then, he should have stayed at home.
(FLAGSTONE *puts on his waistcoat.*)

FLAGSTONE: I think it's a misjudgement.
BENTLEY (*short; ready to leave*): It is.
FLAGSTONE: Someone should tell him.
GORDON (*bowler hat*): Tell who?
FLAGSTONE: Gilbert.
(*General talking.*)
He's only a man like the rest of us. He's not the devil incarnate.
CONYNGHAM: Well, I don't know about you, but he fair scares the living daylight out of me.
PRICE (*large; Northern; reflective; sitting; shirtsleeves*): What about us?
EVANS: Beg pardon, Price?
PRICE: Why can't we speak to Mr Gilbert?
(*Some muttering.*)
Well, we could all go together. There's no reason why we shouldn't. Is there?
LEWIS: Tell a man you admire his lyrics, he can only be gratified.
FLAGSTONE: It's a splendid notion, Mr Price.
EVANS: Well, gentlemen, here's food for thought.
BENTLEY: Indeed, Mr Evans.
(KENT, *a large man and a dandy, sitting next to* PRICE, *has been wiping his hands.*)
KENT (*petulant*): Gentlemen: I have been a chorister in this company for twenty-eight seasons.
(*General groan.*)
It is my intention to remain one for at least another twenty-eight.
LEWIS: I'm sure you shall.
KENT: Be very careful, Mr Price. You must consider yourself, and your position. This is tantamount to professional suicide.
(*Various reactions at once.*)
BENTLEY: I don't think so.
EVANS: Oh, W. J., I do believe that is a little excessive.
(KENT *has picked up his hat, and now proceeds to leave.*)
KENT: Gentlemen, let us repair to the Coal Hole in the Strand.
(*He leaves.*)

CONYNGHAM (*leaving*): Don't be long, chaps!
  (*General chatter.*)
GORDON (*leaving*): Goodnight, gentlemen!
SEVERAL PEOPLE: Goodnight.

In TEMPLE *and* LELY'*s dressing-room.* CARTE, SULLIVAN *and* HELEN *stand looking at* TEMPLE, *who is in his place, still in make-up and costume.* LELY *is mostly dressed.*
CARTE: Take heart, old chum.
HELEN: You're going to be wonderful.
SULLIVAN: Quite so, Dickie.
CARTE: Indeed.
LELY: Och, aye!
HELEN: Is that not right, wee Durward?
LELY: Ach, he'll be grand, Helen.
SULLIVAN: This has taken us all quite by surprise.
HELEN: Mm. And we all know Mr Gilbert.
SULLIVAN: I should have thought it was a fine song.
CARTE: It is a fine song.
HELEN: Mm.
SULLIVAN: Thank you.
HELEN: Is there anything we can arrange for you, Mr Temple?
TEMPLE (*muted*): Hmm? No, thank you, Miss Lenoir. I'll be fine.
CARTE: Well, it's very late. Congratulations, Lely – first class.
LELY (*modest laugh*): Oh, no! (*serious*) Did you think so?
HELEN: Oh, yes.
  (SULLIVAN *dons his top hat.*)
SULLIVAN: Better and better.
LELY: Thank you. *Grazie. Grazie.*
CARTE: The Beefsteak?
SULLIVAN: I'm ravenous.
  (*They leave.*)
HELEN: Gentlemen . . . Goodnight.
LELY: Goodnight, Helen.
CARTE (*in corridor*): Goodnight, Butt.
  (BUTT *is stationed outside the room.*)
BUTT: Goodnight, sir.
SULLIVAN: (*returning*): Dickie. *Courage.*
  (BUTT *tips his hat to* HELEN, *who leaves:* LELY *closes the door.*)

LELY: Well, there you have it, Dickie.
TEMPLE (*deeply upset*): He's an absolute bastard. I knew something of this order was going to happen. I sensed it. I told you so. It really is unconscionably cruel.
LELY: You've missed your last train, Dickie.
TEMPLE: It's too late to telegraph to Mrs Temple now.
LELY: What'll you do?
TEMPLE: Oh, I suppose I shall toddle across the river to my mother's – she never sleeps.
LELY: There's g'aye few like us, and they're all dead. My father used to say that.
TEMPLE: Laughter. Tears. Curtain.
(*Long pause.*)

Next afternoon. The Savoy Theatre. GILBERT *proceeds up the backstage stairs, greeting waiting choristers as he goes.*
GILBERT: Good afternoon, Bovill.
BOVILL: Good afternoon, Mr Gilbert.
GILBERT: Miss Langton-James.
MISS LANGTON-JAMES: Good afternoon, Mr Gilbert.
MISS RUSSELL: Good afternoon, Mr Gilbert.

GILBERT: Good afternoon, Miss Russell.
KENT: Good afternoon, sir.
GILBERT: Good afternoon. (*to* RHYS) Good afternoon, Rhys. Good heavens!
PRICE: Good afternoon, Mr Gilbert.
GILBERT: Good afternoon, Price.
(*On the landing, by a door signposted 'To the Stage',* PRICE *is waiting with a dozen or so fellow choristers – ladies and gentlemen.*)
PRICE: Might you, er, spare us a moment of your time, please?
GILBERT: Yes, of course – that's why we're here. We're about to rehearse.
PRICE: Please, Mr Gilbert, sir.
GILBERT: Yes, Price – what is it?
PRICE: We, er . . .
GILBERT: Mmm?
PRICE: The . . . ladies and gentlemen of the chorus . . .
(*He looks further up the stairs.* GILBERT *does the same, and sees even more choristers.*)
GILBERT: Yes?
PRICE: Concerning Mr Temple's song, sir.
GILBERT: Ah, the Mikado's song!
PRICE: Yes, sir.
GILBERT: And what of that mercifully released aberration?
PRICE: We all consider it a very fine song, sir.
FLAGSTONE: Indeed we do.
GILBERT: Gratifying, I'm sure. But that must be a matter of opinion, mustn't it, Price?
PRICE: Yes, Mr Gilbert, but . . . we believe it a great loss.
FLAGSTONE: A terrible loss.
GILBERT: Do you?
PRICE: Yes, sir.
FLAGSTONE: We do, sir.
MISS CARLISLE: Especially after all our extremely hard work, and of course Mr Temple . . .
GILBERT: I'm really very sorry for you, but as we all know, it's an unjust world!
FLAGSTONE: We all feel it would have been of great benefit to the opera.

MISS KINGSLEY: And that perhaps it should be a matter for the audience to decide.
GILBERT: Is this the considered opinion of you all?
PRICE: It is, sir.
(*Several people corroborate this, speaking at once.*)
KENT: I am not party to this, Mr Gilbert.
GILBERT: Ah, Mr Kent. As ever, the sole voice of reason. Temple, what do you make of this occurrence?
(TEMPLE, *who has only just arrived, takes off his hat.*)
TEMPLE: I do beg your pardon, Mr Gilbert. But I have absolutely no idea what is taking place.
GILBERT: There has been a request that your song be reinstated.
TEMPLE: Ah! . . . Ah.
GILBERT: A most forceful request, I have to say.
(GROSSMITH *arrives.*)
GROSSMITH: Afternoon! Afternoon! Do clear the way! (*He sees* GILBERT.) Oh – beg pardon, sir.
GILBERT: This is surprising indeed, ladies and gentlemen. (*Pause.*) And somewhat overwhelming. (*Pause.*) Temple . . . would you be prepared to sing the song at this evening's performance?
TEMPLE: Yes, sir, I would.
(*A long, tense pause.*)
GILBERT: Then please be so good as to do so.
(*Spontaneous laughter. Some people clap. Much chatter. Several young ladies shout, 'Hip! Hip!' – and there is a chorus of 'Hoorah!' Music cue 15 starts. Then over the hubbub*:)
Rehearsals will commence in five minutes! Seymour, where's D'Auban?
BOVILL: Congratulations, Temple!
TEMPLE (*overwhelmed*): Thank you.
LELY: Dickie! Dickie!
(*Much general jubilation as everybody moves towards the door to the stage.*)

GILBERT's *house. The oak-panelled hall.* GILBERT *rushes out of his study, wearing his full dress suit. He is hotly pursued by* PIDGEON, *who is carrying* GILBERT's *hat, cloak and cane.* MRS JUDD *and the*

MAIDSERVANT *peep round a corner.*
GILBERT: Right you are, Pidgeon, come along! Make haste!
PIDGEON: Sir . . .Sir, it's seven o'clock, sir . . .
GILBERT: One moment . . . (*He turns round abruptly, and heads back towards the study.*)
KITTY (*unseen*): Oh – there you are, Willie!
(*Just as he reaches the study door,* GILBERT *changes course again, and charges off in another direction, still pursued by* PIDGEON. KITTY *joins in the pursuit. She is in her evening gown.*)
Willie! *Willie!*
PIDGEON: The carriage is waiting, sir! Sir . . .
(GILBERT *reverses direction again, and* PIDGEON *follows: then, just by* MRS JUDD *and the* MAID, GILBERT *swings round yet again.*)
GILBERT: Out of my way, Pidgeon!
PIDGEON: I do apologize, sir.
(*Now* GILBERT *goes out through a door.* PIDGEON *follows.* KITTY *stops, and shouts through the doorway.*)
KITTY: Willie – we must be leaving! (*sighing, to the women*) We don't want to be late. (*She joins them.*)
MRS JUDD: You look beautiful, madam.
KITTY: Oh, thank you, Mrs Judd. Oh, it's most pleasant to be appreciated.
(*She leaves the hall. As she goes . . .*)
MAIDSERVANT: Don't worry, madam.
(*This earns a stern look from* MRS JUDD. *They remain at attention. Music cue 15 ends.*)

The Savoy auditorium. The band is tuning up. The audience in the cheaper seats in the gods is already in place, and the stalls are beginning to fill.

Outside GROSSMITH's *dressing-room.* COOK, *in his bowler hat, is waiting on his stool.* SULLIVAN *arrives in his dress suit.* COOK *gets up.*
SULLIVAN: Good evening, Cook.
COOK: Good evening, sir.
(*He tips his hat.* SULLIVAN *nods enquiringly in* GROSSMITH's *direction.* COOK *shrugs subtly.* SULLIVAN *shrugs equally subtly, and goes to the door. He knocks.*)

GROSSMITH (*from within*): Come in.
  (SULLIVAN *opens the door and goes in.*)
SULLIVAN (*from within*): Gee-Gee.
GROSSMITH (*from within*): Arthur.
  (COOK *sits down. The band can still be heard tuning up.*)

A few minutes later. Fully made up as Ko-Ko, and wearing his under-costume (and his pince-nez), GROSSMITH *is sitting in front of his mirror, drinking a cup of tea. Lots of pictures of him around.* SULLIVAN *sits beside him with a glass of whisky.*

SULLIVAN: Your very good health. (*He raises his glass and downs the Scotch. Music cue 16 starts.*)
GROSSMITH: Yours too, Arthur. Splendid piece. (*Sipping his tea.*)
SULLIVAN: Thank you. We shall both be splendid tonight. (*He puts down the tumbler.*)
GROSSMITH: Too many words. (*A nervous laugh.*)
SULLIVAN: I thought I'd just pop in.
GROSSMITH: Much appreciated. So very frightened of losing
  . . . One had to stay by the door, don't you know.
SULLIVAN: I beg your pardon?
GROSSMITH: Fifty pounds per week isn't too much to ask . . .
  Behaves more like a man than a woman.

SULLIVAN: Gee-Gee: try to remember to breathe properly.
GROSSMITH: Yes, yes, yes, yes. This year – next year. Too much *noise*!!
SULLIVAN: George: shall be fetch you a doctor?
GROSSMITH: I know doctors. Coming in here, picking and fussing over one. Magnetizing the children. (*'Sorcerer' gesture.*)
SULLIVAN: We shall have a great triumph, you know.
GROSSMITH: What is the time, by the way?
(SULLIVAN *takes out his pocket watch.*)
SULLIVAN: A quarter past.
GROSSMITH: Ooo-er . . .
SULLIVAN: The dreaded hour approaches. Now: take a deep breath.
(GROSSMITH *does so.* SULLIVAN *joins him.*)
And again.
(*They inhale and exhale together.*)
Very good.

Another dressing-room door. GILBERT *raps on it with his cane. He is wearing his top hat and cloak.*
JESSIE (*from within*) Who is it?
GILBERT: Gilbert!
JESSIE (*from within*): Oh, do come in.
LEONORA (*from within*): Come in, Mr Gilbert.
(*The dresser,* EMILY, *opens the door.* GILBERT *hovers in the doorway.* JESSIE *and* LEONORA *stand side by side. Both are made up.* JESSIE *is wearing her kimono, but* LEONORA *is in her dressing-gown.*)
GILBERT: A brief intrusion.
(*Music cue 16 ends.*)
JESSIE: How are you, Mr Gilbert?
GILBERT: As well as any condemned man can expect!
(LEONORA *giggles.*)
How are you, ladies?
LEONORA: Oh, a little anxious, Mr Gilbert.
GILBERT: Ha! You have every right to be anxious, under the circumstances.
JESSIE: I don't suppose you'll be with us this evening?

GILBERT: Indeed not, Jessie – why on earth should I want to consort with the foe?
JESSIE: Oh, but I'm quite sure we shall have a great success, Mr Gilbert.
LEONORA: Mm.
GILBERT: I wish I possessed your confidence. (*He coughs.*) Well, Jessie . . . *bonne chance!*
   (*He lurches over, and kisses her on both cheeks. He doesn't kiss* LEONORA.)
JESSIE: Thank you.
GILBERT: And you, Tortoise.
LEONORA: Thank you, Mr Gilbert.
GILBERT (*mumbling*): Very good.
   (*He backs out nervously, coughing and touching his hat. Then he disappears down the corridor.* EMILY *closes the door.*)
LEONORA: I shall put on my kimono now, please, Emily.
EMILY: Oh, very well, Miss Braham.
   (*She opens the door and goes out.* JESSIE *paces nervously. Music cue 17 starts.*)

Outside GROSSMITH's *dressing-room again.* CARTE *and* HELEN *arrive briskly.* COOK *gets up.*
CARTE: Good evening, Cook.
COOK: Sir.
CARTE: Is Mr Grossmith respectable?
COOK: I'm afraid not, sir.
   (CARTE *knocks on the door. No reply.*)
CARTE: We'll return later, George.
   (CARTE *and* HELEN *leave.* COOK *touches his hat.*)
GROSSMITH (*from within*): Oh, thank you.
   (COOK *sits down.*)

Moments later – still outside Grossmith's dressing-room. GILBERT *arrives.*
GILBERT: Good evening.
COOK (*touching his hat*): Sir. Er – em . . .
   (GILBERT *knocks on the door with his cane.*)
GROSSMITH (*from within; tetchy*) No, Cookie!
GILBERT: Gilbert.

GROSSMITH (*from within*): Oh, beg pardon, sir.
GILBERT: May I come in?
GROSSMITH: I'm in my birthday suit.
  (*We see him: he isn't – he's fully clothed.*)
GILBERT: Ah! (*To* COOK) Are we not receiving?
COOK: No, sir.
GILBERT: Mm. Good luck, Grossmith! And be careful with the sword. (*He begins to leave.*)
GROSSMITH (*rolling up a sleeve*): Righto!
  (*In the corridor,* GILBERT *collides with* SHRIMP.)
GILBERT: Walk, boy! (*He stomps off.*)
SHRIMP (*touching his cap*): Yes, sir. Permission, Mr Cook?
COOK: Permission withheld, sir. On your way.
SHRIMP: Thank you, sir. Good luck, sir.
  (*He leaves.* COOK *knocks on* GROSSMITH*'s door.*)
COOK: Five minutes, sir.
  (*Music cue 17 ends.* GROSSMITH *puts away a hypodermic syringe and closes its box. He has just injected himself. The mark is on his arm. There are lots of them. He presses a towel on it, and closes his eyes while the drug takes effect.*)

GILBERT *comes out of the stage door. He scowls up and down the street briefly. Then he strides off into the night. A dog barks near by.*

Later that evening. The Mikado *in performance, Act 2. The* CHORUS *of Japanese schoolgirls and noblemen marches downstage in a block. Then they progress formally to the right of the stage, and stand in three lines. As they begin to sing, four Japanese guards appear, wearing samurai helmets and carrying long pikes. The audience is thoroughly enjoying the show.*

CHORUS (*sings*):
> Miya sama, miya sama,
> On n'm-ma no mayé ni
> Pira-Pira suru no wa
> Nan gia na
> Toko tonyaré tonyaré na?

(*The music continues. The guards take up their positions round a sort of raised Japanese gazebo with doors. The* CHORUS *kneels. The doors open, and* TEMPLE *appears as the Mikado, followed by* ROSINA BRANDRAM *as Katisha.* TEMPLE *stands imperiously, surveying all.* ROSINA, *behind him, is expressionless.*)

CHORUS (*sings*):
> Miya sama, miya sama,
> On n'm-ma no mayé ni
> Pira-Pira suru no wa

Nan gia na
Toko tonyaré tonyaré na?
(*Fashionable ladies in the audience fan themselves.* TEMPLE *flicks open his huge black fan.* SULLIVAN *is conducting. The Japanese-style 'Miya sama' music gives way to a rum-ti-tum beat.* TEMPLE *and* ROSINA *come down the steps and take centre stage.*)

TEMPLE (*sings*):
From ev'ry kind of man
Obedience I expect;
I'm the Emp'ror of Japan –

ROSINA (*sings*):
And I'm his daughter-in-law elect!
He'll marry his son
(*Flicking red fan.*)
(He's only got one)
To his daughter-in-law elect!

TEMPLE (*sings*):
My morals have been declared
Particularly correct;

ROSINA (*sings*):
But they're nothing at all, compared
With those of his daughter-in-law elect!
Bow – Bow –
(*They all bow.*)
To his daughter-in-law elect!
(*They all kneel and sing.*)

CHORUS (*sings*):
Bow – Bow –
To his daughter-in-law elect!
(*They bow again as she passes them. She joins* TEMPLE *up the steps. He descends again.*)

TEMPLE (*sings*):
In a fatherly kind of way
I govern each tribe and sect.
All cheerfully own my sway –

ROSINA (*sings*):
Except his daughter-in-law elect!
As tough as a bone,

(*Flicking red fan.*)
    With a will of her own,
    Is his daughter-in-law elect!
TEMPLE (*sings*):
    My nature is love and light –
    My freedom from all defect –
ROSINA (*sings*):
    Is insignificant quite,
    Compared with his daughter-in-law elect!
    Bow – Bow –
    (*They do so.*)
    To his daughter-in-law elect!
    (*They all sit up and sing.*)
CHORUS (*sings*):
    Bow – Bow –
    To his daughter-in-law elect!
    (ROSINA *joins* TEMPLE *up the steps. Now the music gives way to the introduction to the restored Mikado's Song.*)
TEMPLE (*sings*):
    A more humane Mikado never
    Did in Japan exist –

Music cue 18 starts. Meanwhile, somewhere in London, GILBERT *prowls down a dark, dank passage. We hear the sounds of bottles breaking, chains clinking, a dog barking, a man shouting and a baby crying.* GILBERT *passes several shadowy figures. Suddenly, a filthy dishevelled hag grabs him by the arm.* GILBERT *tries to break free.*

GILBERT: Get off!
    (*She rests her head on his shoulder. She is mad.*)
MAD WOMAN (*Irish accent*): Be good. Be good.
GILBERT: What're you do – ?
MAD WOMAN: I'm good. I'm good.
GILBERT: Get your hands off me!
MAD WOMAN: Oh, don't rub your smell off on me!
GILBERT: You stinking bitch!
MAD WOMAN: Help!!
GILBERT: Just let me go – !
MAD WOMAN: Oh, you're a lovely big boy. How old are you?

GILBERT: Don't you touch me!
  (*He breaks free and rushes off. She shouts after him.*)
MAD WOMAN: Who made the world?! Arsehole!!!
  (*In a side street, men run past* GILBERT *at breakneck speed, holding on to their hats. They are pursued by a four-wheeled carriage. A church bell chimes ominously . . . Music cue 18 ends.*)

Back at the Savoy, SULLIVAN *conducts. The* CHORUS *is still where it was.* TEMPLE *and* ROSINA *are sitting on the dais on seats.* JESSIE *and* BARRINGTON *stand in front of the* CHORUS *facing* TEMPLE. GROSSMITH *shuffles forward and bows to the monarch.*
GROSSMITH (*sings*):
  The criminal cried as he dropp'd him down,
  In a state of wild alarm –
  With a frightful, frantic, fearful frown,
  I bared my big right arm.
  (*He bares it.*)
  I seized him by his little pig-tail,
  And on his knees fell he,
  As he squirmed and struggled,
  And gurgled and guggled,

> I drew my snickersnee!
> My snickersnee.
> (*He is a little shaky in his singing.* SULLIVAN *gives him a worried look.*)
> Oh, never shall I
> Forget the cry,
> Or the shriek that shriekèd he,
> As I gnashed my teeth,
> When from its sheath
> I drew my snickersnee!
> (*He pulls out his fan as though it were the snickersnee [dagger].*)

CHORUS (*sings*):
> We know him well,
> He cannot tell
> Untrue or groundless tales –
> He always tries
> To utter lies,
> And ev'ry time he fails.
> (GROSSMITH *shuffles backwards to take up a position with* JESSIE *and* BARRINGTON, *but he accidentally bumps into* BARRINGTON. SULLIVAN *clocks this, and is concerned.* JESSIE, *as Pitti-Sing, shuffles forward, bows, and takes centre stage.*)

JESSIE (*sings*):
> He shivered and shook as he gave the sign
> For the stroke he didn't deserve;
> When all of a sudden his eye met mine,
> And it seems to brace his nerve;
> For he nodded his head and kissed his hand,
> And he whistled an air, did he
> As the sabre true
> Cut cleanly through
> His cervical vertebrae.
> His vertebrae.
> (*The Mikado smirks, and nods approvingly. Katisha observes this disdainfully.*)
> When a man's afraid,
> A beautiful maid
> Is a cheering sight to see;

>   And it's oh, I'm glad
>   That moment sad
>   Was sooth'd by sight of me!
> CHORUS (*sings*):
>   Her terrible tale
>   You can't assail
>   With truth it quite agrees:
>   Her taste exact
>   For faultless fact
>   Amounts to a disease.
>   (JESSIE *shuffles back, bowing, and is replaced by*
>   BARRINGTON, *as Pooh-Bah. He bows and sings.*)
> BARRINGTON (*sings*):
>   Now though you'd have said that head was dead
>   (For its owner dead was he),
>   It stood on its neck, with a smile well bred
>   And bowed three times to me!
>   It was none of your impudent off-hand nods,
>   But as humble as could be;
>   For it clearly knew
>   The deference due
>   To a man of pedigree!
>   Of pedigree.
>   (*Members of the audience, who are following the words in a
>   libretto, turn over the page in unison.*)
>   And it's oh, I vow,
>   This deathly bow
>   Was a touching sight to see;
>   Though trunkless, yet
>   It couldn't forget
>   The deference due to me!
> CHORUS (*sings*):
>   This haughty youth,
>   He speaks the truth
>   Whenever he finds it pays:
>   And in this case
>   It all took place
>   Exactly as he says!
>   (BARRINGTON *has joined the other two. All three sing with the*

CHORUS.)
ALL (*sing*):
> Exactly, exactly, exactly
> Exactly as he says!
> (SULLIVAN *brings the music to an end. Loud applause.*
> SULLIVAN *is delighted.*)

A little later. The Mikado *finale. The principals are grouped in a row across the stage, with the* CHORUS *behind them.* JESSIE *sings to* ROSINA.

JESSIE (*sings*):
> For he's gone and married Yum-Yum –

ALL (*sing*):
> Yum-Yum!

JESSIE (*sings*):
> Your anger pray bury,
> For all will be merry,
> I think you had better succumb –

ALL (*sing*):
> Cumb-cumb!

JESSIE (*sings*):
> And join our expressions of glee!

GROSSMITH (*sings to* ROSINA):
> On this subject I pray you be dumb –

ALL (*sing*):
> Dumb-dumb!

GROSSMITH (*sings*):
> Your notions, though many,
> Are not worth a penny,
> The word for your guidance is 'Mum' –

ALL (*sing*):
> Mum-mum!

GROSSMITH (*sings*):
> You've a very good bargain in me.
> (*Everybody sings and dances. Much fancy fan-work.*)

ALL (*sing*):
> On this subject we pray you be dumb –
> Dumb-dumb!
> We think you had better succumb –

>   Cumb-cumb!
>   You'll find there are many
>   Who'll wed for a penny,
>   Who'll wed for a penny.
>   There are lots of good fish in the sea,
>   There are lots of good fish in the sea,
>   There are lots of good fish in the sea,
>   There are lots of good fish in the sea,
>   In the sea, in the sea, in the sea, in the sea!
>   (*A new tune . . .*)
>
> LELY (*sings*):
>   The threaten'd cloud has pass'd away,
> LEONORA (*sings*):
>   And brightly shines the dawning day;
> LELY (*sings*):
>   What though the night may come too soon,
> LEONORA (*sings*):
>   We've years and years of afternoon!
> SIBYL, LELY, BARRINGTON, BOVILL (*sing*):
>   Then let the throng
>   Our joy advance,
> LEONORA, JESSIE (*sing*):
>   Then let the throng
>   Our joy advance,
> SIBYL, LELY, BARRINGTON, BOVILL (*sing*):
>   With laughing song
>   And merry dance.
> LEONORA, JESSIE (*sing*):
>   With laughing song
>   And merry dance.
> ALL SIX (*sing*):
>   Then let the throng
>   Our joy advance
>   With laughing song
>   And merry dance –
>   With laughing song
>   And merry dance;
>   With laughing song . . .
> EVERYBODY (*sings*):

With joyous shout,
With joyous shout and ringing cheer,
Inaugurate, inaugurate their new career!

With joyous shout and ringing cheer,
Inaugurate their new career!
With joyous shout and ringing cheer,
Inaugurate their new career!

With laughing song
And merry dance.
With laughing song
And merry dance.
With song and dance!!!
(*The music continues. Everybody dances vigorously. The show ends with a big bow. Huge applause.* SULLIVAN *beams with delight, and bows. The principals all shuffle backwards upstage as the curtain is lowered. The folk in the gods cheer.* SULLIVAN *leaves the pit. The curtain is raised again. Everybody bows. The applause continues.* LEONORA *and* LELY *take their bow.* SEYMOUR *is in his usual prompt-corner position in the wings. He shouts an instruction.*)
SEYMOUR: Pish, Peep.
(SEYMOUR *and* BOVILL *take their bow.*)
Mikado.
(TEMPLE *takes his bow. The applause increases.*)

In the stage-door corridor. BARKER *is waiting.* GILBERT *appears.*
BARKER: Ah!
(*He rushes off towards the stage.* GILBERT *follows.*)
GILBERT: How bad was it?
BARKER: Utterly dreadful! – a joke: I jest!
(*Some theatre workers pass by.*)
GILBERT And Grossmith?
BARKER: A lamentable spectacle.
GILBERT: Mm.
(GILBERT *has removed his hat and cloak.* BARKER *takes them.* CARTE *arrives.*)
CARTE: Are you ready, Gilbert? (CARTE *leaves.*)

GILBERT: Ready for what? The gibbet?!
(GILBERT *and* BARKER *follow* CARTE.)

The applause in the theatre continues. GILBERT *and* CARTE *join* SEYMOUR *in the wings.* SEYMOUR *is directing the stage-hand who raises and lowers the curtain.* GILBERT *is obviously extremely jumpy.*
SEYMOUR: And . . . full company. Ladies and gentlemen: bow!
(*The full company bows.*)
Thank you very much.
(GILBERT *has a quick look to make sure* SULLIVAN *is on the other side of the stage. Then he goes on, meeting* SULLIVAN *in the middle.* SULLIVAN *is holding his white conducting gloves in one hand. He bows with great charm and confidence.* GILBERT *is stiff, nervous and self-conscious. Endless applause.* SULLIVAN *holds out his hand to* GILBERT. *They shake hands.*)

Later. KITTY*'s bedroom.* KITTY *is sitting up in bed, wearing her nightdress. Her hair is down.* GILBERT *sits on the end of her bed, still in his first-night apparel.*
GILBERT: There's something inherently disappointing about success.
KITTY: Climax and anticlimax, Willie.
GILBERT: I don't quite know how to take praise. It makes my eyes red.
KITTY: But it must be rather pleasant to receive it, nonetheless.
GILBERT: I suppose so. If one feels one deserves it.
KITTY: I don't think anyone would deny that you deserve it, Willie.
GILBERT: I know my limitations.
KITTY: I should rather like to be an actor, upon the stage.
GILBERT: An actor?
KITTY: Yes. Wouldn't it be wondrous if perfectly commonplace people gave each other a round of applause at the end of the day? (*She claps enthusiastically.*) 'Well done, Kitty. Well done!' (*She laughs.*)
GILBERT: Well done, Kitty! *Bravo! Encore!*
KITTY: Thank you, Willie. (*Pause.*)
GILBERT: Well, you must be tired.
KITTY: Must I?

GILBERT: I shall leave you to your beauty sleep.
KITTY: No, don't go. (*Pause.*) Any thoughts racing round in that old brain of yours?
GILBERT: Thoughts of what nature?
(*A long pause. She looks at him with great gravity. Perhaps she almost says one thing, but then changes her mind, and says something else . . .*)
KITTY: Concerning your next piece.
GILBERT: Oh! That monster! No, not as yet.
(*Pause.*)
KITTY: Perhaps you should do something completely and utterly different and unusual.
GILBERT: Such as what?
KITTY: Oh . . . well, I don't know.
GILBERT: Come along – suggest something!
KITTY: Oh . . .
(*Pause. She giggles.*)
Well . . . you should have a young and beautiful heroine . . .
GILBERT: Mm.
KITTY: Who grows old and plain. And as she gradually becomes older and older, the ladies' chorus becomes younger and younger. (*She laughs.*)
GILBERT: Ah, topsy-turvy.
KITTY: Yes.
(*Pause. Music cue 19 has started.*)
GILBERT: And how would it commence, this comic opera of yours?
KITTY: With the gentlemen's chorus, of course. (*Pause.*) A chorus of fat leeches.
GILBERT: Leeches?
KITTY: Yes. No, they'd be gentlemen . . . and – and they'd be in their carriages, and they'd be . . . rushing across the stage; the horses would be galloping across the stage, and the ladies would be chasing after them, endeavouring to talk to them, but they wouldn't be listening – they'd all be far too busy.
(*Pause.*)
GILBERT: Mm. Expensive to stage.

KITTY: And there'd be dozens of doors and ticking clocks on the stage. And he's made a vow to give her the key, but he never does.

GILBERT: And who might he be?

(*Pause.*)

KITTY: He's her husband, I suppose . . . the hero. No, not the hero. Anyway, one day . . . no: late one night, she suddenly decides to try the door, and it opens.

GILBERT: Ah, so it wasn't locked, after all.

KITTY: And she climbs up the stairs, and there, on the sands, are hundreds of nannies, all pushing empty perambulators about!

(*Pause.* GILBERT *is affected by this. Tears have appeared in* KITTY's *eyes. Music cue 19 ends.*)

And every time she tries to be born . . . he strangles her with her umbilical cord.

(*Long pause.*)

GILBERT: Mm . . . I shouldn't imagine Sullivan'd much care for that.

(*Kitty is in pain. Music cue 20 starts.*)

SULLIVAN's *bedroom. Day. He is sitting up in bed in his nightshirt.*

Beside him, in full evening wear, is FANNY, *sitting on the bed.*
SULLIVAN: I'm proud of myself, triumphant, exhilarated, exhausted, revived, and . . . fed up to the back teeth with these wretched kidneys.
FANNY: Poor old thing.
(*She touches him gently as he re-arranges himself.*)
Arthur, an old demon has come back to haunt us at a most unwelcome time.
SULLIVAN: What on earth d'you mean?
(FANNY *places her hand on her stomach.*)
Oh.
FANNY: I didn't want to tell you.
SULLIVAN: Are you sure?
FANNY: Yes.
SULLIVAN: How long have you known?
FANNY: Ten days.
SULLIVAN: Oh, Fanny. (*Pause.*) I shall make the arrangements.
FANNY: That won't be necessary. I couldn't go through that again.
SULLIVAN: I'm sorry that you have to.
FANNY: I've made my own arrangements.
SULLIVAN: Have you?
FANNY: Someone has been recommended to me. (*She puts on her gloves.*) After all, it is 1885, Arthur. I love *The Mikado*. You've put everything you are into it. You light up the world. You can't help it.
(*She kisses him on the cheek.*)
I must fly.
(SULLIVAN *ponders things. Music cue 20 ends as we go into the next scene.*)

LEONORA *is alone in her dressing-room. She is fully made up and dressed as Yum-Yum. She gazes intently at her reflection in the mirror. She has had a great deal to drink, and she is holding a glass of sherry. She quotes Yum-Yum's soliloquy from* The Mikado, *Act 2.*
LEONORA: Yes, I am indeed beautiful! Sometimes I sit and wonder, in my artless Japanese way, why it is that I am so much more attractive than anybody else in the whole

world. (*She leans forward.*) Can this be vanity? (*She blows herself a kiss.*) No! Nature is lovely, and rejoices in her loveliness. I am a child of Nature, and take after my mother.
(*She drinks some sherry and continues to gaze at herself. There is a hint of tears in her eyes. We hear the introduction to the song that follows.*)

LEONORA *is standing alone on stage in a spotlight. The scene starts in a close-up, and during the song the camera cranes back over the orchestra and the audience, ending in a long-shot from the back of the circle.*
LEONORA (*sings*):
    The sun, whose rays
    Are all ablaze
    With ever-living glory,
    Doe not deny
    His majesty –
    He scorns to tell a story!
    He don't exclaim,
    'I blush for shame,

So kindly be indulgent.'
But, fierce and bold,
In fiery gold,
He glories, all effulgent!

I mean to rule the earth,
As he the sky –
We really know our worth,
The sun and I!
I mean to rule the earth,
As he the sky –
We really know our worth,
The sun and I!

(*She moves coyly into a slightly different position on the stage.*)
Observe his flame,
That placid dame,
The moon's Celestial Highness;
There's not a trace
Upon her face
Of diffidence or shyness:
She borrows light
That, through the night,
Mankind may all acclaim her!
And, truth to tell,
She lights up well,
So I, for one, don't blame her!
Ah, pray make no mistake,
We are not shy;
We're very wide awake,
The moon and I!
Ah, pray make no mistake,
We are not shy;
We're very wide awake,
The moon and I!
(*We cut to black. Music cue 21 starts.*)

A caption:

Gilbert & Sullivan wrote five more operas, including *The Yeomen of the Guard* and *The Gondoliers.*

Another caption:

Sullivan only wrote one grand opera, *Ivanhoe.*

Although moderately successful at the time, it is now mostly forgotten, and isn't as much fun as *The Mikado.*

THE END

The Music Cues

Carl Davis's score is all drawn from Arthur Sullivan.

1. *The Yeomen of the Guard*. The 'Private Buffoon' theme from the overture.
2. *The Yeomen of the Guard*. The 'Wooer Goes A-Wooing' theme from the overture.
3. *The Long Day Closes*. Song by Sullivan.
4. *The Yeomen of the Guard*. ' 'Tis Said That Joy in Full Perfection' from the Finale, Act 2.
5. *The Grand Duke*. 'As O'er our Penny Roll We Sing' from Act 1. This piece is often known as the 'Habanera'.
6. *The Grand Duke*. The Dance from Act 2, followed by 'My Lord Grand Duke, Farewell' from Act 1.
7. *The Grand Duke*. 'When You Find You're a Broken-down Critter' from Act 1.
8. *Ruddigore*. Opening bars of overture and of 'I Once Was as Meek as a New-born Lamb' from Act 2.
9. *Ruddigore*. Same as cue 8.
10. *The Mikado*. 'Our Great Mikado, Virtuous Man' from Act 1.
11. *Patience*. 'The Soldiers of our Queen' from Act 1. 'So Go to Him and Say to Him' from Act 2.
12. *The Merchant of Venice*. 'Danse Grotesque' from Sullivan's incidental music to Shakespeare's play.
13. *The Gondoliers*. 'Take a Pair of Sparkling Eyes' from Act 2.
14. *The Yeomen of the Guard*. The 'Private Buffoon' theme (see cue 1).
15. *The Grand Duke*. The 'Habanera' (see cue 5).
16. *The Yeomen of the Guard*. 'I Have a Song to Sing, O!' from Act 1 and Act 2.
17. *The Yeomen of the Guard*. The 'Private Buffoon' theme (see cues 1 and 14).
18. This is really a piece of pure dramatic film music by Carl Davis. But if you listen carefully you will hear the 'More Humane Mikado' theme, which Temple has just sung at the end of the preceding scene.

19 *TheThe Yeomen of the Guard.* ' 'Tis Said That Joy in Full Perfection' (see cue 4).
20 *Iolanthe.* 'He Loves' from Act 2.
21 *The End-title Music:*
   a) *The Mikado.* 'The Sun Whose Rays' from Act 2.
   b) *The Pirates of Penzance.* 'Climbing Over Rocky Mountains' from Act 1.
   c) *The Grand Duke.* The 'Habanera' (see cues 5 and 15).